Sacred Sight

Finding Hope Through Heartache

Glenda Love Durano

Published by Legacy Press
Your life tells a story; we can help you write it.
LegacyPress.org

Printed in the United States of America

ISBN (print): 978-1-957026-31-2
ISBN (eBook): 978-1-957026-32-9

Cover design and interior layout and design by Nelly Murariu @PixBeeDesign.com

This book is based on true events. It reflects the author's present recollections of experiences over time. Some events have been compressed, and some dialogue has been recreated.

Most people mentioned in this book have given permission to use their names, except for a few who have not returned our correspondence. Even in these few instances, we believe all mentioned will be pleased to know their place in our story.

To all involved in this story—friends and family who supported us, strangers and acquaintances who prayed for us, and physicians and care-givers who helped Amberle find her way back to health—whether recorded in the pages of this book or not (yes, I am talking about YOU), our family will always be grateful for your love, kindness, and generosity. You are a tangible expression of God's grace.

So we fix our eyes not on what is seen, but on what is unseen,
Since what is seen is temporary, but what is unseen is eternal.

2 Corinthians 4:18 (NIV)

CONTENTS

FOREWORD

Have you ever seen time move backward? A blur of color, a blizzard of sound, and all that was lost is new again. Life rewinds and the question of why is finally answered—puzzle pieces come together, and you begin to see a purpose in the pain. Reason. Redemption. Revelation.

This is a story of dreams, anger, questions, and discovery. A tale of suffering, pain, survival, and rebirth. It's the story of losing a sense in order to find an ability to perceive. And this story is not over. The rewinding has just begun.

Going blind is a strange sensation. It's all at once subtle and dramatic, devastating and . . . fine. As my vision has fluctuated and hung in the balance, I've stumbled through the dance of grasping onto the imperceptibly small things—wrinkles on a forehead, twinkling of an eye—and letting the seemingly large things lie—proclamations of a future lost, fears of all the dark beyond. I'm relearning how to walk, and leaning less on sight and more on faith that something even exists to walk into.

I was twenty-one years plus twelve days old when I was admitted to a Burn ICU for an autoimmune disease that melted away my skin and organ linings. I was only twenty-one, but I surely thought I had the next sixty years of my life figured out. I was only twenty-one, dreaming of the adventures of a lifetime, but not knowing the adventure that life itself would be.

One time, I was walking in a neighborhood, feeling the ground ahead of me with my white cane to avoid breaking an ankle on an uneven slab of sidewalk when a little boy playing in his front yard, mistaking my cane for a metal detector, called out, "Are you looking for treasure?"

Yes, I am looking for treasure. And I'm beginning to find it.

Amberle Durano Brown

PREFACE

I believe in miracles—those inexplicable times when circumstances line up too perfectly to be coincidence. Getting a flat tire less than a quarter mile from the only tire store in the county. Having our mortgage rate drop when our bank account was doing the same. Receiving a text from a friend at just the right time. Big or small, I count each one as a miracle—because God answered my prayers *exactly* the way I wanted.

Until one day, He didn't.

Have you been there? Life is rolling along, then in a split second, your life is changed forever. An accident. A diagnosis. A disaster. A betrayal. And pain like you've never felt before.

Where is God? Where's my Miracle-maker?

That was my question when my twenty-one-year-old daughter landed in the ICU. But there was no answer to that question—or any of my questions.

As a Christian, I knew the answer in my head. God was with me. God cared. God loved me. But I wanted to feel it in my heart.

So, I kept praying.

I knew God could heal her, but He didn't. That's when I discovered the greatest miracle of all—God's unconditional love—a love that in forty years of being a Christian, I'd never really known. Sure, it was there all the time, but I didn't know it. A love not based on circumstances or blessings or because "the Bible tells me so," but a love based on relationship. A love that transforms faith into sacred sight and manifests hope through heartache.

For a long time, I refused to accept "no" as the answer to my prayer. I was blinded by the answer I wanted—supernatural healing—and, as a result, I couldn't see the answer was already there. I wanted God to do something in the here and now, but God wanted to do something for eternity, something "immeasurably more than all we ask or imagine" (Ephesians 3:20 NIV).

If I learned anything from this journey, it's that prayer changes things. Every. Single. Time. Sometimes circumstances and sometimes lives.

So, pray. For big and small miracles. But especially for the ability to surrender your need to "have it your way"—to know why and how and when and what if—in exchange for the opportunity to increase your faith, find your hope, and know Him more. And if your miracle doesn't happen, know it's because God has something better for you, something unimaginably better.

Perhaps instead of giving you an answer, God wants to give you Himself.

Glenda Love Durano

Chapter One

In the Beginning

I stood at the kitchen table, my fingers hovering above my laptop's keyboard. Maybe I could find an answer online. I didn't have one in my head, and I needed one—desperately. That's what you do when a doctor tells you he's putting your twenty-one-year-old daughter into a medically induced coma.

"Is it Stephen's Johnson or Steven Johnson?" I yelled to my husband. "More than one Stephen? With a *ph* or a *v*?"

"I don't know. The doctor just called it SJS. Let's go. I'll put the bag in the car."

My husband was in bulldozer mode: get it done. On this night, October 11, 2012, that meant getting to Fort Worth, Texas, as soon as possible. There were no more flights out of Albuquerque, so driving was the best alternative.

The ER doc had seen only seen a couple of cases of SJS in his decade of experience, so he wasn't positive about the diagnosis. SJS is rare—one in a million—but whatever it was, he said, the disease was in the early stages, so Amberle would probably be fine.

Probably? That's not something you tell a parent who's six hundred miles away.

His bedside manner failed. "A medically induced coma will give her a better chance."

Of what? I wanted to ask. *A better chance of what?* But fear melted the words in my mouth.

I had spoken to Amberle last night, right before she posted that goofy picture of herself and her friends in the ER. *Does it really take four girls to take Amberle to the emergency room?* But then it made sense. They probably stopped to get ice cream on the way because life is one big party with Amberle.

Don't get me wrong. Amberle has a serious side. She's brilliant. Highly analytical. But with her, life is a celebration.

Over the last few days, Amberle hadn't been feeling well. Pain in her lower GI tract. Hives. Swelling. Trouble breathing. She couldn't get in to see her doctor, and the campus clinic had run some inconclusive tests. As any nursing student would do, she self-diagnosed, ultimately deciding she was having an allergic reaction. What began as a low-grade fever had spiked to and was holding at 104 degrees. Even with that, an ER doc at a different hospital had sent her home the night before.

Not this time.

I hit return on my keyboard and found some answers. I wished I hadn't.

Stevens-Johnson Syndrome. More than one Steven, with a *v.*

I scrolled down the page. Horrifying images appeared. People burned beyond recognition—looking like the walking dead.

No, God. Please, no.

I had my answer. I wanted to give it back, but it was too late. My unsubstantiated fear morphed from fiction to fact.

Answers can do that. They make the unimaginable imaginable.

Dee and I got in the car. He routed us to the hospital in Fort Worth and told me to sleep until we got to Amarillo, but when I closed my eyes, images of blackened bodies appeared. I texted a few friends and relatives: "Amberle admitted to hospital. Something called SJS. On our way to Fort Worth. Please pray."

I researched SJS on my phone before we lost cell service:

- † Stevens-Johnson Syndrome: A rare and serious disorder of the skin and internal mucous membranes usually caused by an allergic reaction to a medication
- † Begins with flu-like symptoms, followed by a rash that erupts into blisters causing the skin and organ linings to eventually peel off
- † Converts to toxic epidermal necrolysis (TEN) when more than 30 percent of the skin is affected
- † Life-threatening
- † No known cure

What do you do with that? I swallowed the lump in my throat and reminded myself everything would be fine. It had to be. That was the plan. The plan Amberle had carefully executed over the last fourteen years. Completing her nursing degree at TCU was the capstone that would allow her to fulfill her dream of becoming a missionary nurse—a desire she'd had since she was seven years old.

"I know what I want to be when I grow up," my second-grader said as I tucked her under a fluffy eyelet comforter.

"What do you want to be, honey? A princess?"

"No, Mommy. That's silly. I want to be a martyr."

As part of our bedtime ritual, every night before we prayed, we read a selection from *Foxe's Book of Martyrs*. Granted, reading stories about the torture and death of early Christians probably wasn't the best way to ensure my two daughters' sweet dreams, but both loved Jesus and seemed inspired by the true tales.

The next evening, when Amberle mentioned her newfound ambition again, her dad and I explained our concerns about her chosen calling. We suggested an alternative: being a missionary. Our young evangelist refused to be sold on the idea until we told her about "unreached people groups," communities distinguished by a language or culture that are less than 2% Christian. That sounded appealing, like an almost impossible challenge—bringing the gospel to groups of people with few or no Christ-followers.

Later, when Amberle discovered indigenous missionaries were the most effective evangelists among unreached people groups, she asked God to make her a member of such a group, a bold request for an upper middle-class Filipino-American. Even at a young age, Amberle believed nothing is impossible with God (Luke 1:37).

When she was nine, Amberle decided nursing would be her vehicle to the mission field. Throughout elementary and high school, she volunteered at hospitals, went on mission trips, and even earned her licensed practical nurse certification at age seventeen, four months before she could legally practice. As a Chancellor's Scholar at Texas Christian University, Amberle excelled academically and socially. Her idea of a good time was serving meals at the homeless shelter or helping refugees resettle.

Now, this Stevens-Johnson Syndrome threatened both my child's dream and her life. I thought I'd found an answer, but all I'd really found was the source of more questions.

Questions with no answers.

Chapter Two

Into the Unknown

At 3:00 a.m., my cell phone rang, interrupting an intermittent nap. It was my older daughter, Christina, calling from Israel.

"Mom, what's wrong with Amberle? I saw something on Facebook that said she's in the hospital. I tried to call her, but she's not answering her phone. Why didn't you call me? What's wrong?"

I tried to sound calm. "Honey, we don't know anything yet. We're on our way to Fort Worth, and as soon as we find out something, we'll call you. I didn't want to worry you."

"Well, it didn't work. When I saw the post, I panicked."

Christina and Amberle were close, and I could tell Christina's feelings were hurt. "I'm sorry. I just know you're busy. Besides, we really don't know anything yet."

"You can call me anytime, day or night. If I'm in class, I'll step into the hall. OK, Mom?"

"OK," I promised. "Now, tell me about you. How's the Hebrew coming?" Christina was two weeks into a master's program at the University of Tel Aviv. The first month consisted of a Hebrew language intensive.

Christina said she was enjoying the language and the culture, but the newfound skill she was most proud of was learning how to find the closest bomb shelter when the air raid alarm sounded. "It happens several times a week. It's really interesting."

Interesting? Reading a book is interesting. Cowering in a bomb shelter is alarming.

My mind spun: one daughter in the hospital, another in a war zone. I tried to listen as Christina spoke for a few more minutes, but my mind refused to focus. When we said our goodbyes, I promised to keep her updated.

†

We arrived in Fort Worth early enough to miss the morning traffic and the rain from the evening before. Exiting the freeway, we spotted a Starbucks across from the hospital. "Can we grab a quick coffee?" I asked. We turned into the parking lot.

Standing in line, I heard a familiar voice, "Glenda? Dee?" It was Ron Pitcock, Amberle's honors advisor.

Before I could ask why he was there, he spoke up. "Lyndsey called me last night when they admitted Amberle." Lyndsey was Amberle's best friend. Three years earlier, they'd met during freshman honors orientation and bonded immediately through a common faith. Dr. Pitcock had been at the hospital since 1:00 a.m. and filled us in on the overnight details. Amberle's condition was worse. "Several of her friends were so concerned they took turns sleeping on the floor next to her bed in the emergency ICU."

We took our coffees and drove two blocks to the hospital's parking garage. Dr. Pitcock escorted us through a maze of stark, windowless hallways and halfway-open doors. The smell of antiseptic mingled with the scent of patients' breakfasts.

Grabbing my husband's hand, I forced a smile as the sliding glass door to the emergency ICU opened. A dozen pairs of eyes landed on us, and in the silence, I heard the beeping of a machine I knew was keeping my daughter alive.

One by one, the dozen or so individuals introduced themselves. Some we knew; others we didn't. There was Dr. Paulette Burns, the dean of the nursing school; Dr. Diane Hawley, Amberle's nursing advisor; and Dr. Susan Weeks, another nursing professor—all well-loved by our daughter. I'd never met the representatives from student services, academic affairs, or student health.

What were they doing here at 7:00 a.m. on a Friday morning? These people weren't just being nice, and they weren't just doing their jobs either. Something in the way they shook our hands—almost as if they were expressing condolences—concerned me. Obviously, they knew something we didn't.

"I'm sorry, but I have to go," Dr. Pitcock said. "I have an eight o'clock class. Keep me posted. Amberle's very special—to all of us."

We said goodbye, and Dee chatted with some of our new acquaintances. Dr. Hawley touched my arm. "Would you like to see her?"

"Yes, I would."

Dr. Hawley guided me to a side room and opened the door. I stepped inside. Amberle's skin was blotched with large red marks, and tubes entangled her body. *This couldn't be my daughter, could it?*

I took a moment to breathe and found some words. "Hi, sweetie. Dad and I are here. We sure do love you, and we're going to get this all figured out. I promise." I felt like I was speaking more to myself than her, and somewhere inside, I wondered if I'd just lied. *Would we be able to figure it out?*

I looked over my shoulder. The attending physician was talking to Dee. "Here's what I think is happening . . ." His uncertainty was unsettling.

The doctor painted a grim picture and reiterated the facts we'd read on the internet. Then he added, "It's possible, because it's progressing so quickly, this could actually be toxic epidermal necrolysis. That's what it's called when more than thirty percent of the body is affected, and unfortunately, TEN, as we call it, has a much higher mortality rate for its victims. About thirty percent."

An audible gasp came from the non-nursing staff.

"Regardless, we don't have the expertise or the equipment to handle it here. You need to get her to a Burn ICU as quickly as possible. Parkland Hospital in Dallas is closest, but they only have twelve beds, and they were full last night. You may need to medevac her to San Antonio."

Within a couple of hours, we were following an ambulance to Parkland, thanks to a bed being vacated earlier that morning. I was grateful we weren't winging our way to San Antonio. Shelby, one of Amberle's friends, offered us a room for the weekend at her parents' home in Dallas.

Dr. Hawley met us at the hospital where one of her former students checked Amberle in. After a flurry of activity, Amberle was whisked away to the Burn ICU. "They'll take good care of her," Dr. Hawley assured us. "They're going to bring her out of her coma so they can assess her condition. One of my favorite alums, Kelly, works in the Burn ICU, and she's agreed to keep a close eye on Amberle. Let's grab a quick bite right now, so you can be ready to see her when the doors open."

We had no clue what she meant.

"Visitors to the Burn ICU are limited: two people per patient during each fifteen-minute visitation period. You'll have to wear a mask, gloves, and scrubs when you see Amberle. With burns or conditions in which the skin sloughs off like SJS or TEN, the chance of infection is high." Dr. Hawley tried not to sound too clinical, but she knew too much not to.

My mind swirled as our footsteps echoed down the hallway leading to the cafeteria. Finally, I broke the silence, "Dr. Hawley?"

"Please, call me Diane."

"All right. Diane, how long does this SJS or TEN or whatever-it-is normally last?"

I was afraid of the answer, and by the ensuing pause, I could tell she was too.

"It's impossible to say. But you should be thinking in terms of weeks, not days."

I heard the words, but they made no sense.

We gulped down our dinner and returned to the entrance of the Burn ICU. "Put on some scrubs," Dr. Hawley instructed Dee and me, "so you'll be ready to go in at six."

As I covered my clothes with blue scrubs, I felt like I was getting ready to walk into an episode of *Grey's Anatomy.* We were almost ready to enter the Burn ICU when the elevator door opened, and three of Amberle's friends, Lindsey, Cheraya, and Shelby, came into the waiting area. In the midst of midterms, they'd driven forty-five minutes to see Amberle.

We knew the rules. Fifteen minutes of visitation six times a day. Two people at a time. When Dr. Hawley explained the visitation procedure to the girls, their faces dropped. They knew there wasn't enough time for everyone to see Amberle, so they told us to give Amberle a hug. We nodded and said we'd do our best to make sure they could see her too.

When the doors opened, a nurse showed Dee and me to Amberle's room—one of a dozen surrounding a large nurses' station. Amberle was in bed, entwined by tubes and wires that allowed nurses to monitor her vital functions. The light from the sunset filtered through three large windows on the far side of the room. On the other side was a supply cabinet and the door to a private bath. The nurse, Kelly, had written her name and the date, October 12, 2012, on the whiteboard. Amberle opened her eyes when we entered the room. Her eyes were covered with a protective membrane, so I wasn't sure how well she could see. Because she was intubated, she couldn't talk. I bent down and hugged her. Struggling to hold back tears, I explained that she was in a Burn Intensive Care Unit at Parkland Hospital in Dallas. She was confused. So were we.

Without warning, Dr. Hawley and Amberle's friends entered the room. "It's all right," Kelly said. "Just keep the noise down."

"It pays to have friends in high places," Diane winked.

Dr. Hawley immediately began asking Amberle yes-or-no questions to assess her level of consciousness, which was amazingly high considering the drugs in her system.

Suddenly, Amberle became agitated and started making frantic movements, like a desperate game of charades. After a few minutes, we realized she was concerned about missing a babysitting job that evening. Fortunately, Lindsey had already hacked into Amberle's calendar and canceled her appointments for the weekend.

Our precious fifteen minutes finished all too quickly, and the following two and a half hours dragged by as we waited for the final visitation of the day. Lindsey, Cheraya, and Shelby returned to Fort Worth, but Dr. Hawley stayed until one of the physicians gave us an update. His conclusion? We'd have to wait and see. My conclusion? Not knowing seemed worse than knowing.

Dr. Hawley said she would press harder tomorrow if they didn't give us some idea of what was going on. She promised to return in the afternoon after her classes but would call Kelly in the morning for an update.

Dee paced up and down the hall, making phone calls to his subcontractors to ensure the work on the home he was building was being completed properly. Dee had recently started working again after the 2008 recession robbed him of three and a half years of employment. It had been a difficult time of testing, but I had a feeling what was coming would be much worse. We weren't just talking about losing money; we were talking about losing a life.

Word spread quickly about Amberle's condition, and her Facebook page exploded with hundreds of prayers and well wishes. I was so inundated by texts and emails that I gave up answering them. I only returned phone calls from friends and family, but I hated doing it because they all had the same question: How is she?

I had no answer.

When I called Christina, she begged to talk to her sister. "Call me the next time you're in her room and she's awake. I don't care if it's the middle of the night here. I need to talk to her."

I promised Christina if Amberle was awake at nine o'clock, I'd call again, but Amberle wasn't. Although she was technically sound asleep, Amberle's body was wide awake. The monitors indicated her heart rate was around 120, meaning it was struggling to keep her body alive.

Dee and I stood by her bed and prayed. There was nothing else we could do.

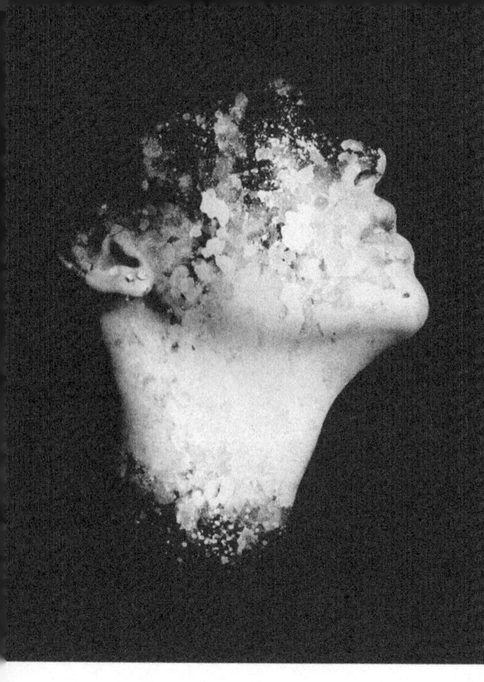

Chapter Three

The Question

We tossed and turned most of the night, sleeping in the guest room at Shelby's parents' home.

We couldn't drag ourselves to the 6 a.m. visitation but arrived in plenty of time for the 8:30. Kelly was off for the weekend. Amberle's male nurse assured us she was being well taken care of but couldn't give us any specifics from the doctors' rounds that morning. I could tell Amberle wasn't quite as comfortable with him as she'd been with Kelly.

As promised, we made a quick Skype® video call to Christina. She was clearly disturbed to see Amberle so incapacitated. Nevertheless, Christina faked normalcy by providing us with a monologue about her adventures at graduate school amid the Israeli air raid sirens. It was easier to discuss the possibility of thousands of foreigners dying than to even think about it happening to her sister.

The waiting room was like an airport on Saturday—people coming and going, each with a purpose. Dee and I smiled at strangers and a few of them asked, "Do you have someone in the Burn ICU?" We explained we did, but when they asked what happened, we could only respond that doctors thought it might be SJS, but they weren't sure. Nobody had heard of Stevens-Johnson Syndrome.

Some of the people had been visiting family members in the Burn ICU for months, and their weekend visits were routine. Many of them knew each other and asked how their father, brother, or uncle was doing. Almost all the patients in the Burn ICU were men who'd been injured in some sort of accident, and everyone agreed the healing process was painfully slow.

Amberle was the exception in gender and age—except for a four-year-old girl, Eva, who had suffered massive burns in a house fire. Eva's father was a truck driver, and her extended family lived far away so she rarely received visitors. The nurses had unofficially adopted Eva and took turns pulling the toddler around the unit in a little red wagon while they tended to other patients.

At least a dozen friends visited Amberle on Saturday. We were grateful for their support, but a part of us wanted to have Amberle all to ourselves—especially since we knew we'd have to return to Albuquerque soon. The weekend nurse stuck closely to the rules so only two visitors were allowed at one time in each of the six fifteen-minute visitation periods. In order to accommodate all the guests, most visitors went in pairs for about seven minutes each. Several friends waited hours to see her.

We waived most of Saturday's visits with Amberle so she could see her friends. Because she was still intubated, visits consisted primarily of one-way conversations and prayers. Sometimes, Amberle asked for a pen and scribbled a note requesting a Scripture to be read or a song to be played on her iPod—anything to escape the pain. When friends exited the unit, we asked for an update. Dr. Hawley visited in the afternoon and, as promised, pressured the attending nurse for more information. A cadre of doctors had made their rounds early that morning—a bit surprising for a Saturday—but apparently Amberle's case was unique.

About midday, Amberle's nurse told us he'd given Amberle the ability to administer her own pain medication, but she wasn't using it, even though her condition was growing worse.

When we visited Amberle at two o'clock, we asked her why she was withholding pain medications from herself. To our surprise, instead of a shrug, Amberle began communicating through sign language. I wasn't very good at signing; it had been years since I'd used it, but we stumbled through a short conversation. As a nurse, Amberle knew the dangers of becoming addicted to pain medication, and it wasn't going to happen to her. In a situation where it seemed like she had no choices, Amberle discovered a way to feel empowered.

We also asked Amberle what she wanted us to tell everyone who was asking us how she was. She thought for a moment then signed six letters: j-o-y-f-u-l. We knew she was directly referencing one of her favorite Scriptures, Romans 12:12 (NIV): "Be joyful in hope, patient in affliction, faithful in prayer." Unlike us, her belief was becoming stronger through this trial; ours was crumbling.

Our sense of helplessness was magnified by the fact that Dee and I needed to drive back to Albuquerque in a few days. Dee had to get back to work, and I was directing weekly rehearsals for our megachurch's annual Christmas production with a hundred and twenty school-aged kids. Plus, as an independent education counselor, this was my busiest time of year, helping students with college applications. I called my older sister Diane and asked if she'd drive from Tulsa to Dallas to stay with Amberle on Wednesday. She was happy to oblige, but my eighty-one-year-old mother also insisted on coming. We were concerned Mom would be more of a liability than an asset, but I was too exhausted to argue. Dee and I would leave Wednesday morning at eight, and Diane and Mom would arrive in Dallas around ten. I would return to Dallas on Friday.

Throughout the day, Dee and I were inundated by phone calls, emails, and texts from friends who wanted to know about Amberle's condition. Most people asked about the *what*—clarification of what was happening and how they could effectively pray—but behind every situational question was a spiritual one—the question no one dared to ask: *why?*

Then came the text from our nephew: "Hi Uncle Dee. Mom told me Amberle is in the hospital. I'm sorry. She's always been good and didn't do anything wrong, but now she might die. Why did God let this happen?"

Why?

That was the question everyone wanted to know the answer to, but no one wanted to ask. Asking why opened the reality of the spiritual realm—a part of our lives that, up until now, had been entirely pleasant and seemingly, reciprocal. We loved God, and He loved us, and life was good. But now our status quo was shaken, and we were confused. This scenario didn't fit into our box of being a child of God, and it simply wasn't fair.

The way I thought, we'd held up our end of the bargain. We'd obeyed God for decades: praying, going to church, giving tithes and offerings, reading the Bible, leading ministries. And we were up to date with our "spiritual insurance premiums." (You know, that unspoken agreement that so many of us have with God: If I do *x*, then He'll do *y*.)

We didn't know how to answer our nephew because we were just as confused as he was. Maybe more. We believed God is a good God (Psalm 107:1); He has good plans for us (Jeremiah 29:11); and He works everything together for good for those who love Him (Romans 8:28). We believed that, but at this moment, our God didn't seem to exist. Nothing about this situation was good.

When it was finally time for the nine o'clock visitation, Dee and I were the only ones in the waiting room. We were relieved to have fifteen minutes alone with her, and thankfully, Amberle was awake.

"What do you want me to say?" Dee asked Amberle when he told her about her cousin's question. "He's asking why this happened, and I don't have an answer."

Amberle was pensive. Slowly, she signed: b-e-c-a-u-s-e. She pointed up.

"God?" I asked. She nodded.

She crossed her hands over her chest in an *x*.

"Love?"

Another nod. Then she pointed to herself.

"Because God . . . loves . . . me?" I asked. "That's what you want us to say?"

Amberle nodded.

What we didn't know was that a few days earlier, Amberle had prayed, "Father, put to death my impatience and selfishness." (Those were the precise words found months later in her prayer journal.)

God had not brought this catastrophe upon my daughter, but in this broken world, He allowed it. Fortunately, Amberle knew the truth: in His love, God blesses us, and in His love, He refines us.

It wasn't the drugs in Amberle's system that created her response. It was the Holy Spirit in her heart. Although Dee and I heard her words—God's words, really—they didn't make sense. They were true, but the situation made it difficult to believe them.

Before we left the hospital that evening, the nurse told us Amberle was breathing well enough to have her breathing tube removed. We were delighted with the glimmer of hope. He said he would do it after we left, and if there was any problem, he would call us.

Chapter Four

The Nightmare

Sunday came early. At three a.m., we received a phone call. "He's hurting me," a raspy-voiced Amberle cried. "Help me, please." The call came from a number we didn't know. Amberle didn't have her phone in the hospital—she'd lost it a few days before getting sick. (Losing her phone was a regular occurrence.) We dressed quickly, and when we got to the hospital, we headed directly into the Burn ICU. No visitation rules were going to keep us out. When we arrived at Amberle's room, the night nurse stopped us.

"She wanted to call you, so I let her borrow my phone. She's fine, but since she's been restricting her own meds, it hurt when I removed her breathing tube and changed her dressing."

In her room, Amberle was on the verge of sleep and didn't remember calling us. She'd increased her self-medication, and we were glad she was going to rest. We headed back to the house to do the same.

On Sunday morning, we received an answer we didn't want. Amberle's condition had deteriorated to toxic epidermal necrolysis (TEN). Now she faced a thirty percent mortality rate from organ malfunction, infection, or pneumonia.

Two-thirds of Amberle's skin was covered with palm-sized blisters, and the proliferation showed no signs of stopping. Amberle's nurse reminded us we were only seeing a fraction of the battle her body was fighting. The lining of every organ inside Amberle's body was being eaten away as well—eyes, ears, nose, throat, lungs, liver, stomach, intestines—every system was jeopardized, as if she were being burned from the inside out.

Amberle's friends were in church Sunday morning, so Dee and I had some time alone with Amberle. Although she slept most of the time, we treasured being with her. When Amberle woke up, even though she was hoarse from being extubated, we Skyped® Christina. That afternoon, a group of Amberle's friends arrived in the waiting room with several dozen cards and a pile of gifts, including a soft, blue blanket and a container of homemade cookies.

"Who made the cookies?" I asked.

"Hunter," Lindsey replied. "He's had a crush on Amberle for about a year, but can't get up the courage to ask her out."

"I've known him since middle school," Shelby added. "He goes to UT Arlington. Plays golf. I think his roommate Cameron helped too."

"That's nice. What about the blanket?"

"That's from Hunter's mom. She thought it would be softer than the hospital bedding."

Although I'd never met these people, I was grateful for their kindness.

Because Dee and I had spent time with Amberle, we let her friends have all the afternoon visits. Visitors were an important part of Amberle's recovery process—they kept her spirits up—but now, some of the doctors felt she was spending too much time with friends when she should be resting. The nurse said they might curtail her visits—or at least limit the people who were allowed to see her.

Amberle didn't remember much about the emergency room, so now, even though it hurt to speak, she asked her friends to fill in the details. Their eyes filled with tears as they told of their constant prayers, calling Dr. Pitcock, and sleeping in the ICU.

Suddenly, Amberle remembered a conversation she'd overheard when the doctors intubated her in the ER.

"You were awake?" her friends asked.

"I tried to move, to yell for help, but my body wouldn't cooperate. That tube hurt so much." Then, almost clinically, she added, "I must have a high tolerance to anesthesia."

During one of the evening visits when Dee and I were the only ones there, Amberle grilled her nurse regarding her medication and her condition as if she were a nursing preceptor instead of a patient.

When Amberle finished the interrogation, the nurse replied, "You really know your stuff. You'll make a great nurse someday."

Amberle smiled, but I knew something bothered her.

"I don't get it," she said after the nurse left the room. "I still know things, but I don't know how. This all seems so real, but I'm sure it isn't. I hope I wake up soon. I don't like this dream."

That's why Amberle seemed so calm. For her, this was a bad dream, not reality. Amberle closed her eyes and drifted into a drug-induced sleep while Dee and I remained in a living nightmare.

†

Monday and Tuesday moved like wet cement. The doctors became more concerned, but wouldn't share much information, even with Dr. Hawley. Amberle floated in and out of sleep during visitation times, and we, along with her friends, were satisfied just to be in the same room with her.

I received at least 100 messages each day asking about Amberle. One of the hospital social workers saw me replying to the emails and texts and suggested I blog about Amberle's illness on a website called *Caring Bridge*. "It's a great way to keep family and friends updated, and it will be a lot easier for you."

I enjoy writing so I decided to give it a try, hoping that putting my thoughts on paper would help me process what was happening. In my first blog post, "Just the Facts," I wrote about Amberle's condition and the grim statistics surrounding TEN. I shared Amberle's determination to be joyful in spite of the circumstances and compared the facts of the situation with the truth of God's love. Every encouraging word was written as much for me as it was for the readers.

I published the first blog on Tuesday, October 16, Christina's twenty-fourth birthday.

Because of her raw throat, Amberle couldn't speak, so our Skyped® birthday wishes to Christina were pretty short. After Christina updated us on life in Israel, she asked if she could talk to Dee and me privately.

"I think I should come home," Christina said. "I want to help Amberle."

"And quit graduate school?"

"I'd have to for now, but I could come back later. I just want to help Am."

"What can you do here that you can't do there?" Dee asked.

"I don't know. Just be there? Look, I'm willing to come. I don't have to go to grad school right now."

We spoke for about ten minutes, and ultimately decided there wasn't anything Christina could do in Dallas that she couldn't do in Tel Aviv. It seemed like the only thing anyone could do was pray. I'd already decided I would spend five days in Dallas and two days in Albuquerque until this situation ended. Dr. Hawley, my sister Diane, and several friends in Dallas agreed to be with Amberle on the days I couldn't be in Dallas.

Looking back, although this was a providential decision in many ways, not allowing Christina to come to Dallas was a choice that negatively impacted our family for years to come.

†

On Wednesday morning, although everything in me wanted to stay with Amberle, I knew we had to leave. Dee and I kissed Amberle goodbye during the 8:00 a.m. visitation, and I promised to return Friday afternoon. In a way, I was grateful for the membranous lenses protecting her eyes and limiting her sight so she couldn't see the anguish on my face. I felt like I was going away forever.

Before we left, the nurse asked for a list of people who could visit while we were gone. I didn't want to restrict visitation, but the doctors insisted. We provided a list of Amberle's closest friends, Dr. Hawley, my sister, and my mom.

Dee and I didn't talk much on the way home. Every ounce of energy, every prayer, and every thought focused on Amberle. When my sister called to say she and Mom had arrived in Dallas, I was relieved.

I called my clients—families I was helping through the college application process and explained the situation. If an appointment wasn't work-related, I canceled it.

During one phone call, the mother of one of my students asked, "Glenda, have you bought your plane ticket back to Dallas?"

I hadn't.

"We have tons of airline points. May I buy your ticket back to Dallas?"

I barely knew this person outside our client-consultant relationship, and I was so overwhelmed I began to cry. Her offer was the first of dozens of tangible demonstrations of God's love we experienced throughout our journey—many from people we didn't even know.

†

In the middle of the Texas panhandle, my phone rang. "Mrs. Durano, this is Amberle's nurse at Parkland Hospital."

I put the phone on speaker so Dee could hear.

"Amberle's having problems breathing. Her oxygen level is less than ninety percent. We think her lungs and trachea are sloughing, and her airway's blocked by membranes. We need to ventilate her again in order to keep her breathing."

"Yes," I said, trying to sound calm. "What do we need to do?"

"Nothing. There's nothing you can do. I just wanted to keep you posted."

As soon as I hung up, my sister Diane called to say they were indeed going to intubate Amberle. Several of Amberle's friends were also at the hospital.

"You should've heard them," Diane said. "They made a huge deal of making sure Amberle has enough anesthesia. She has great friends."

Diane told me she and Mom had met Dr. Hawley. "I can't believe she drives forty-five minutes each way to see Amberle. She says she tries to visit every day. What a godsend!"

Diane also told me when Dr. Pitcock, Amberle's mentor and honors advisor, had said goodbye to her after his visit, Amberle became agitated and tried to remove her IV and feeding tubes. They couldn't figure out why until Amberle reached toward him. She was begging him to take her home.

My heart imploded as I held back tears. Like my daughter, I wanted to wake up from this nightmare, but I couldn't. As the nurse had said, and as I'd told Christina, there was nothing we could do . . . except pray.

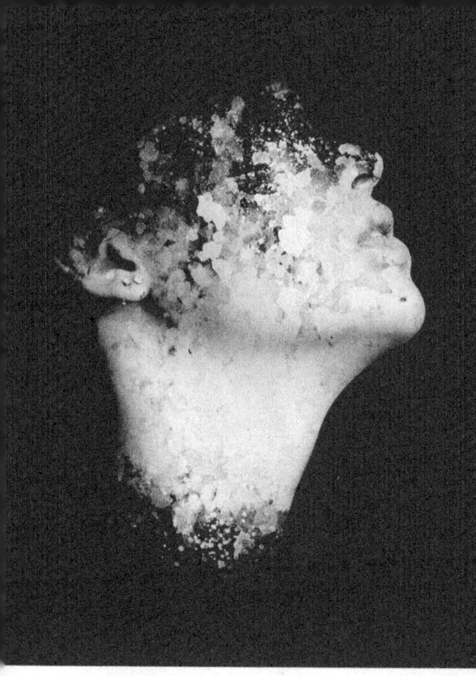

Chapter Five

The Only One

We were exhausted when we arrived home. Our West Highland Terrier, Sarah, trotted out of the laundry room to greet us.

"Looks like Bethany took good care of you," I said, rubbing her neck. Every time we were out of town, our dog-loving neighbor, Bethany, spoiled Sarah. When we left for Dallas, I'd texted her in the middle of the night and asked her to take care of our furry child.

"Go back to sleep," I told Sarah, as Dee and I headed for the bedroom.

I rose early the next morning. I had to go to the store, do laundry, and take care of a dozen things before I returned to Dallas.

I opened the refrigerator. To my surprise, it was full. There was a note from Bethany on the kitchen counter next to some beautiful, fresh flowers: "Welcome home, friend. I got the neighbors together, and we filled your fridge and freezer. We're ready to restock whenever you need us to. Figured you wouldn't have time to cook—and God forbid Dee tries to!"

The freezer and refrigerator were filled with homemade, frozen casseroles and easy-to-warm dishes. Although "there was nothing anyone could do," the little and not-so-little blessings people provided assured us we weren't going through this valley alone.

I walked through the house trying to find where I'd put my phone the night before. When I entered the living room, I stopped. Sitting in a large chair in the corner of the room was a stuffed Tigger—the "bouncy, trouncy, flouncy, pouncy fun, fun, fun, fun, fun" character from A. A. Milne's *Winnie-the-Pooh* series. I collapsed in the chair and held the orange-and-black striped character close.

Our family loves *Winnie-the-Pooh*. When our kids were little, we read the series aloud, and they loved watching the cartoon series. Christina, Dee, and I always identified with the obsessive Rabbit, but not Amberle. Amberle was Tigger—happy-go-lucky—a party waiting to happen, and definitely, as the song says, "the only one." Now, here was Tigger sitting in my living room. It was as if God was saying, "Don't worry. She'll be fine."

When I found my phone, I called Bethany and thanked her for the food, flowers, and taking care of Sarah. "And I love the little Tigger toy!" I said, explaining why the stuffed animal meant so much. "How'd you know?"

"I didn't," Bethany said. "Glenda, I didn't buy that stuffed animal. I found it on the living room floor the day you left."

"That's weird."

"It sure is." She paused for a moment. "You know what I think happened? That first day, I let Sarah out in the morning, and I went back to my house to do some chores. When I returned a few hours later, the back door was open, and Sarah was wandering around the house. I guess I forgot to lock the door. I walked through the house to see if she'd had an accident, and that's when I found Tigger. I put him in the chair since I didn't know where he belonged."

"Well, that explains it," I said. "Thanks a lot."

The mystery was solved. Or was it?

I hung up and texted a picture of Tigger to Christina. "Is this little guy yours?" Christina kept a large basket of stuffed animals on the floor next to her bed. I figured Sarah had grabbed it while she was exploring the house.

"Never seen him," Christina texted.

Weird. Although she hadn't lived at home for several years, Christina knew where everything was in her room. Since Tigger didn't belong to Christina, it must've been Amberle's, which would've been fine except for one thing. Amberle didn't display her stuffed animals the way Christina did. Amberle kept her stuffed animals in a box under her bed.

How was it possible our renegade puppy discovered that particular stuffed animal—the one that represented Amberle to me—among dozens of stuffed animals in a box under Amberle's bed and brought it to our living room so Bethany could place it in the chair where I would see Tigger when I arrived home?

It was not possible. And yet, there it was—a tiger-striped miracle. Was this merely coincidence, or had God stepped into my home to lovingly provide a ten-inch-tall reminder that He alone is "the only one?"

I needed a miracle, so I chose God as the explanation for my Winnie-the-Pooh wonder. Yet, at that moment, for so many things in my life, I didn't just want an explanation. I wanted an answer.

My forty hours in Albuquerque felt like forty days. I spoke to my sister every couple of hours and Dr. Hawley twice a day. The situation changed constantly.

Every day, the physicians told Dr. Hawley that Amberle's condition was peaking, but the next day, more lesions appeared. It was the worst case of toxic epidermal necrolysis they'd ever seen. Since Amberle had been on her back for nearly a week, doctors administered antibiotics to prevent pneumonia. They gave her medication to slow her heart rate and restricted her visitors to family members, Dr. Hawley, and four of her closest friends.

I never felt so helpless in my life, and my cries to heaven bounced back in silence.

I worked with several students on their college applications and planned the next choir practice. My jobs provided a diversion from the guilt I felt over being so helpless.

My supervisor at church, Roxie, a dear friend and mentor, asked, "Can you handle this? If you can't, we'll find a way to make the choir program happen without you. Amberle has to be your priority."

"She is." I told her of my plan to commute weekly.

"If that's what you want to do, that's fine, but we're here to support you, whatever you decide."

†

I arrived in Dallas late Friday afternoon. When I visited Amberle, I was greeted by Kelly, the TCU alum nurse I'd met the first day. Kelly explained that Amberle's breathing tube had just been removed, so she would have additional pain.

"Her body is about eighty percent affected now. It's progressed a lot over the last few days, and we don't know if it's plateaued yet. We thought if Amberle had the same caregiver every day, we could better monitor her condition, so I requested Amberle as my patient when I'm on duty. I think the consistency will be good for her—and that way, I can let Dr. Hawley know about any changes."

"That's great," I said.

"Amberle did show some positive progress regarding her mental state. Early this morning, she asked if she could watch *Finding Nemo*. We thought Eva might watch it with her, but that only lasted about an hour." I'd seen Eva—a shy four-year-old, being pulled in a wagon by the nurses as they cared for the patients.

"Eva's tough to entertain, but I think she's starting to warm up to Amberle. They even did a little physical therapy together this week. Eva hates PT, but when she saw Amberle wiggling her fingers and lifting her arms, she did it too. It was good . . . for both of them."

"Well, it's good to have friends," I said. "And speaking of that, do you know when they'll lift those visitor restrictions? I think Amberle would like to start seeing more people."

"I'll ask about that," Kelly said. "By the way, who is Collin? He isn't on the approved visitor's list, but he's been coming every morning. He asked if he could pray for Amberle during the 6:00 a.m. visitation. Is that OK?"

"Sure, but Collin lives in Austin. He's Lindsey's boyfriend and a good friend of Amberle's."

"Well, I don't know how he does it, but he's been here praying every morning at 6:00 for the last four days."

"That's great. We need all the prayer we can get."

Kelly escorted me into Amberle's room and checked her vital signs while I gave Amberle a hug.

"I don't want to hurt you," I said.

Amberle smiled, glad to have the human contact.

The walls of Amberle's hospital room were plastered with get-well cards, and several stuffed Tiggers sat on the window ledge, gifts from well-wishers who, I assumed, had read my blog post about the stuffed animal incident.

"I decided to display Amberle's cards to remind her how much she's loved," Kelly said. "Hey, Am, I'll be outside if you need me. Like Nemo says, just keep swimming. You're doing better."

I turned my eyes toward Amberle. *Better?* She looked awful to me. Some of her blisters had popped, exposing large, open wounds on her body, and she looked more dead than alive. Nevertheless, I wanted to stay positive. I needed to stay positive.

"I'm glad you watched *Finding Nemo*," I said.

"Yeah, I couldn't really see anything, but at least I could imagine it, and it gave me something to do. Except this time, I felt so sorry for Dory. She reminded me of me. Always in a daze."

"Well, your fog is drug-induced," I said. "And if you weren't on all those meds, you'd be . . ." I chose my words carefully, ". . . a lot worse off."

I read a few Facebook messages to Amberle. "Oh, did you know tonight is homecoming?" I asked. "Look at all the . . ." I caught myself. Amberle had no way to look.

"I know," Amberle said. "I wish I could go."

My jaw tightened, and I held my breath. I wanted to feel sad, but instead, I was angry. *Where was God in this mess? He could fix this. Why didn't He?*

I knew my frustration wouldn't help Amberle, so I controlled myself. "I wish you could go too."

I looked at Amberle's body and wondered how she could bear the pain. "Dad wants to know how you're doing, sweetie. I want to take a picture so he can see for himself. Is that OK?"

Amberle nodded.

Her broad smile, a trademark of Amberle's photographs, was nonexistent, shattered by the pain. As my lens focused on various parts of Amberle's broken body, I wondered if it could get any worse. Thousands of purple sores plastered her body, sores that would eventually erupt into large blisters that would explode, decimating her skin. Dead tissue and open wounds, left in the wake of her body's assault on itself, covered her neck and chest. A clear, heavy gel coated her face to keep the black scar tissue soft so it could be peeled away less painfully by her caregivers.

Visitation was almost over. "Do you need anything before I go?" I asked. "More meds? A cold washcloth?"

"Ice cream," she croaked. A slight smile formed on her lips. Maybe my daughter was doing better.

Eager to provide Amberle with even the smallest pleasure, I asked Kelly if Amberle could have some ice cream. Kelly said anything cold would ease Amberle's throat pain—if she could keep the food down.

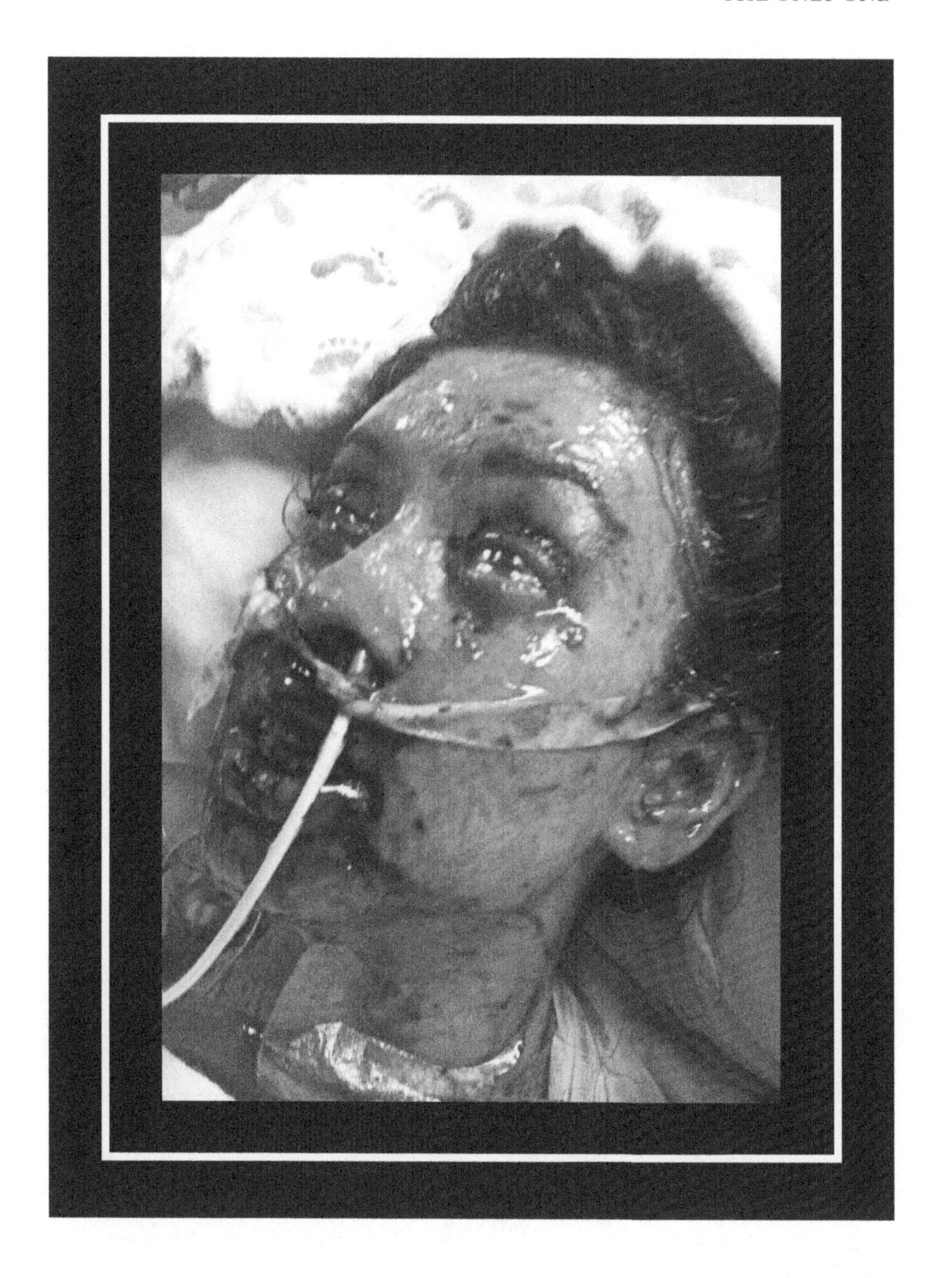

When I left for the evening, Amberle was listening to worship music and sucking on a cherry popsicle.

It almost seemed like she was my daughter again. Amberle: the only one.

Chapter Six

If Anyone Can

Alone in my hotel room, I prayed. I cried. I yelled. I felt like I was falling in slow motion into a bottomless abyss. Before, I'd always been able to fix things and make them right. Or more accurately, God had. Because He loved me. And I loved Him. And that was the deal.

Until that moment, however, I didn't realize how seriously I took that deal and how, deep down, I felt entitled to God's favor. I knew God didn't promise His children an easy journey, but I assumed His sovereignty would offer some protection. That was why I was so offended. *Where was He now?* Part of me believed God couldn't know about our pain (although I knew that was impossible) because surely, if He did, He would save us. But then I remembered Jesus. If God's sovereignty didn't spare His Son's suffering, why would it nullify ours?

There was no deal, and as much as I wanted my good behavior to manipulate God's actions, it didn't. God's actions were motivated by love, not by me. My pride hated to admit it, but I had no control. That's why I was so upset. This wasn't just about circumstances. It was about sovereignty, surrender, and selfishness.

I sat in the darkness, waiting for God to punish me for my lack of faith. But He didn't. Instead, I felt surrounded by love, compelled to release the heavy burden of control. I needed to trust God more than I trusted myself, and I needed to believe what Christ did two thousand years ago was more important than anything He could do today. Accepting God's love meant finding security in Christ's assurance instead of a false insurance based on my behavior.

I asked God to forgive me and to teach me to trust Him. I'd never prayed a more dangerous prayer. I wanted to know who, what, when, where, why, and how this nightmare was going to end. But trusting God meant I had to be OK with not knowing.

†

Amberle's friends took a break from their homecoming activities to visit her on Saturday morning. Kelly was generous and allowed everyone to go in at once as long as we kept the noise to a dull roar.

Amberle's friends talked about their classes, clubs, assignments, and activities. It all seemed so spectacularly boring. So natural. So normal.

I would've given anything for normal.

Collin, Lindsey's boyfriend, was there as well.

"What's this I hear about 6:00 a.m. visitations?" I asked.

"Since most of my work is online, I'm staying with a friend here in Dallas so I can pray with Amberle every morning."

"I can't believe you'd do that."

"Believe it," Lindsey said, taking Collin's hand. "He's a special guy, and he loves Amberle almost as much as I do."

Kelsey, one of Amberle's friends from her nursing cohort, chatted about an exercise they'd done in class. Amberle hung on every word.

"I'm going to have a lot to catch up on," Amberle said. "Can I borrow your notes?"

"Sure," said Kelsey. "You'll be up to speed in no time."

"Hey, Lindsey, have you finished your Fulbright application yet?" Amberle asked.

"I'm going to try to finish it tomorrow so Dr. Pitcock can proof it."

"I still have to work on mine, but at least I already turned in the Marshall application. I think I'll ask Dr. P for an extension on my Fulbright. I don't know if I'll finish in time."

Time. Ours was frozen, but somehow, everyone else's time moved forward. Ten days ago, Amberle's desire to finish her application would've been admirable. Now, it was irrational.

As I watched Amberle's skin disintegrate, I sensed her future dissolving too, and the chasm between what I wanted for my daughter and what I knew to be true widening every day.

†

Sunday morning was quiet. Around 9:00 a.m., Kelly poked her head into the waiting area and motioned me to come.

"What's wrong?" I asked as we headed back toward the Burn ICU.

"Nothing. It's really quiet today, and I thought you'd enjoy some time with your daughter."

"But it's not visiting hours."

"I know," said Kelly. "If the docs come, you can wait outside. I just really think Amberle needs to know you're here today."

I enjoyed our one-on-one time, but the unspoken anxiety and unanswered questions sat like an invisible blanket, smothering our words. It took so much energy to not talk about certain things that we barely spoke at all.

Around noon, one of the doctors came to check on Amberle. I stood up to leave.

"Are you Amberle's mom?" He walked over to shake my hand. "I'm Dr. Kennedy, the ophthalmologist. You don't have to leave. I'm just here to scrape her eyes. This'll only take a minute."

"Scrape her eyes?"

"Yes. Otherwise, they might seal shut. Sorry, this isn't fun."

Amberle groaned.

"I'm sorry, Amberle. I'll try to be quick." The doctor took a scalpel-like instrument from his coat pocket and leaned over Amberle. I couldn't bear to look. Amberle breathed deeply, trying to control the pain. After a few moments, Dr. Kennedy said, "All done. Sorry, Amberle. I know it hurts."

After he left, Amberle sighed, "I hate this, Mom. When can I get out of here?"

I wished I knew.

†

When Amberle's friends visited that afternoon, I decided to grab a bite to eat. As I headed out of the Burn ICU, I saw Dr. Hawley putting on scrubs to visit Amberle.

"Diane," I said, hugging her tightly. "Thank you for keeping me updated while I was gone. I don't know what I would've done without you."

"My pleasure. I enjoyed meeting your mom and your sister, and I know Amberle was glad to have them here."

I invited Diane to join me for lunch. In the cafeteria, I confessed my growing anxiety. "I want to trust God, but it's hard. I want to be OK without any answers, but I need some sort of context so I know what to expect."

Diane thought for a moment before she spoke. "All right, but you need to know this isn't an answer. Experience tells me this is far from over. The blistering hasn't stopped yet, and after it does, it'll take four to six weeks before she's discharged."

"Four to six weeks?" The realization stunned me.

"She should be home by Christmas, maybe even Thanksgiving."

"But what about school?"

"She'll probably have to withdraw and start over. If she's able."

Diane saw the disappointment in my eyes. She touched me lightly on my arm.

"If anyone can do it, it's Amberle."

"But she already completed half the semester."

"I know. But right now, she can't read or write. Amberle has a long way to go to get back to normal. It won't be easy."

I knew she was right.

"Amberle will have a lot of rehab when she gets out of the hospital. This is going to change your family's life."

I let the thought sink in and reminded myself of my commitment to trust God rather than myself.

Diane continued. "What I'm most concerned about is Amberle's mental state; I'm especially concerned about PTSD. Her drug dosage is so high it's likely she won't remember anything about being here. It'll be like a part of her life disappeared. I mentioned that to Lindsey a few days ago, and she said she'd get Amberle a journal for visitors to write in. That way, Amberle can have some sort of record of her time here."

My heart hurt, and my mind was empty. How could I tell Amberle? Diane was kind enough to give me some silence to process our new reality.

After lunch, Diane and I went into Amberle's room. A beautiful journal sat next to Amberle's bed and beside it was a note asking visitors to write a message, favorite Scripture, or prayer. Her friends had returned to campus to study, but several of them had already written supportive words Amberle would find encouraging.

Early that evening, Dr. Pitcock brought a stack of cards from Amberle's friends in the honors program.

When he finished reading them to her, Amberle thanked him. "Dr. P," she said, "I have favor to ask."

"What do you need?"

"Well, I'm not sure if I'm going to finish my Fulbright application on time. I may need an extension. When's the latest I can get it to you?"

Dr. Pitcock looked at me and then Amberle. "Amberle, if anyone is qualified for those fellowships, it's you. But you need to focus on getting well right now. Those applications should be the last thing on your mind. You've hit a bump in the road. You will get better, and then you can do whatever you want. But right now, you need to focus on getting well."

Any sign of hope left Amberle's face, and a lump appeared in my throat.

It was the nicest no I'd ever heard.

Chapter Seven

All We Can Get

On Monday morning, my phone rang. It was an unfamiliar number with a Fort Worth area code.

"Mrs. Durano?"

I vaguely recognized the voice of the caller.

"This is Dr. Chung. I treated your daughter Amberle about ten days ago at Baylor Scott & White All Saints Medical Center. How's she doing?"

I was taken aback by this stranger's interest in Amberle, but I wasn't totally surprised. This was the new normal.

When I told him his original diagnosis of toxic epidermal necrolysis had been proven correct, he was overcome with emotion.

"I wasn't sure. I've worked in the ER for fifteen years, and I've never seen a case that early in development. Normally, TEN is misdiagnosed, so by the time we see the patient, the condition is far more severe. That's why it has a thirty percent mortality rate. It's really miraculous she came in when she did."

I agreed.

"I know this is difficult—seeing your child in such pain and not knowing what's going to happen. But something about your daughter has stayed with me, and I've found myself praying for her over the last week and a half. I hope you don't mind."

"Of course not," I said. "We need all the prayers we can get."

"I'm not going to ask you to stay in touch because I know you have a lot on your plate, but I'll keep checking on Amberle through my connections at Parkland. I really do wish you the best."

"Dr. Chung," I said, hoping to catch him before he hung up. "Thank you for saving my daughter's life."

He paused. "You're welcome. And I'll keep praying,"

I hung up, but I didn't feel alone. By now, I'd seen uncommon tenderness everywhere. People who'd never met Amberle sent messages on Facebook saying they would pray for her or responded to the *Caring Bridge* blog by sending donations via the website. The readers didn't realize the money they gave didn't go to us, but instead, to maintain the *Caring Bridge* site. Still, I appreciated their kindness and their desire to be a part of the healing process. Their hearts joined with ours, and their support encouraged us every day.

When I saw Amberle an hour later, she was alert.

"Eva and I are making plans," she said.

"Oh really? What kind?"

"Halloween. She's going to be Ariel, the little mermaid, and she says I should go as a mummy."

I laughed. It was an allusion to Amberle's bandage-wrapped body, and while there was nothing funny about it, I found myself smiling. In the midst of her pain, Amberle managed to find joy with a four-year-old burn victim who, like her, had suffered without cause.

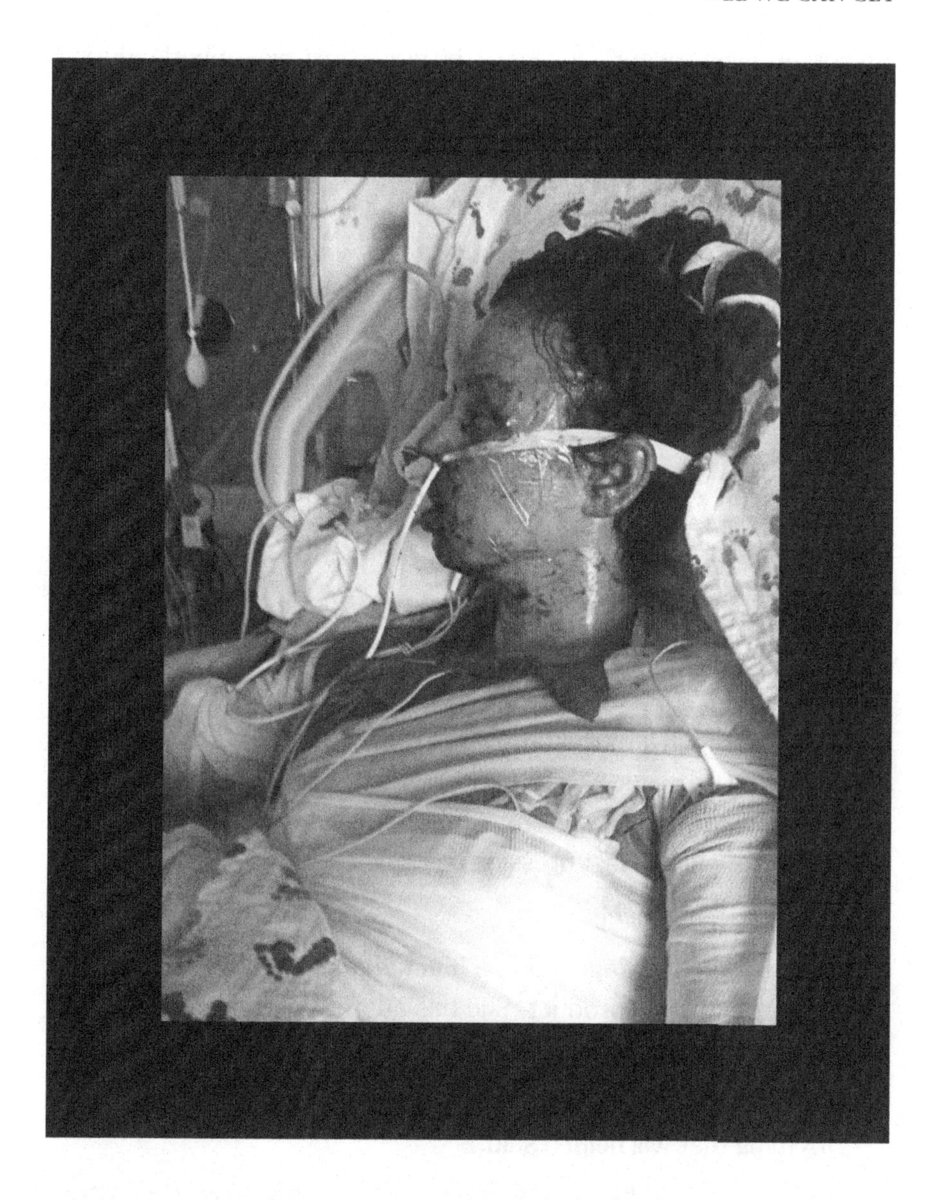

Eva and Amberle had an irrefutable bond. Sometimes, when Eva refused to do her physical therapy, the nurses brought Eva to Amberle's room to play "Amberle Says," a personalized version of "Simon Says." When Amberle waved her arm or kicked her leg, Eva did the same, and in this way, Eva completed her therapy. Nurses used the unique bond to their advantage, even encouraging Eva to be brave "just like Amberle" during her painful burn treatments.

Before visitation was over, I checked Amberle's Facebook page.

"Did you know they're having a prayer vigil for you Tuesday night?"

"I know. Everyone's been so good to me."

Before lunch, in the waiting room, I edited the last of my students' admissions essays. I was glad my students' college applications were almost complete. I had a lot of work to do for children's choir.

"Mrs. Durano?"

I looked up.

"I'm Dr. Wolf."

I'd heard this man's name dozens of times during the last ten days. He and Dr. Arnoldo were the two primary physicians in the Burn ICU.

"I know it's been a hard battle, Mrs. Durano, and we keep thinking Amberle's condition has peaked, but the truth is, it hasn't. She's blistered over nearly 90 percent of her body now, so it has to stop soon. We're doing our best to make her comfortable and expedite her healing. Did she tell you about her last dressing change?"

I nodded. It had been painful.

"Because the bandages did so much damage when we removed them, we tried a new product. She has another dressing change this afternoon, and we're hoping it won't be as painful. This new product is experimental, but we've heard good things about it."

"Anything that will help," I said.

"And I think we'll discontinue those visitor restrictions. The nurses tell me Amberle's mental state is much better when she has visitors, and since we're fighting a battle in both her mind and her body, I think visitors will be beneficial."

I agreed, and I knew Amberle would too.

"Amberle tells me she wants to be a missionary."

"Yes. It's been her dream since she was seven years old."

"Well, I want you to know I'm going to do everything in my power to make sure that dream comes true." He smiled and moved toward the door.

"Thank you. A lot of people are praying for both you and Amberle every day."

"Great. We need all the prayers we can get."

†

Amberle's dressing change was catastrophic. The new product stuck to her skin more than the first one—something we thought was impossible—and when it was removed, it ripped away every inch of Amberle's flesh.

"Pray hard," Kelly told me when she came to the waiting room to give me an update. "Her blood pressure's really low, and her temp's spiked to 104."

The nurses increased Amberle's anesthesia to such a high level that they woke her every hour to make sure she was still conscious. At 6:00 that evening, I was allowed to see her. Amberle was moaning in her sleep, having a nightmare.

"Should I wake her?" I asked the night nurse.

"No. She needs as much rest as she can get. We have to wake her every two hours throughout the night for eyedrops, so I don't think you should wake her unless you have to. Maybe she'll be awake for the 8:00 p.m. visitation."

I returned to the waiting room. A little before eight, two of Amberle's friends arrived. I told them to visit Amberle first, and I'd go in after them.

When they got to Amberle's room, the door was closed, and the nurse wasn't at her station, so they assumed the nurse was inside with Amberle. While they were waiting, they heard a loud "thud" followed by what sounded like Amberle screaming in pain. They opened the door and found Amberle writhing on the floor in a pool of blood. Several nurses heard the cries and rushed into her room.

Amberle's friends ran to get me in the waiting area, and, between sobs, tried to explain what happened.

I hurried to her room without stopping to put on scrubs. Amberle was curled up in a fetal position on the cold linoleum floor, moaning and crying, surrounded by several nurses.

"What happened?" I yelled.

"Mom, help me."

I ran to Amberle's side. "I'm here, baby. I'm here."

"I don't how she jumped out of her bed," the head nurse explained, "but she did. You're one strong girl, Amberle."

"I was only gone for a minute," said the night nurse.

While they mopped up the pool of blood, I stroked Amberle's head and silently prayed.

"It's OK, baby," I kept repeating. "It's OK."

"I don't think she broke anything," said one of the nurses, "but it looks like she lost everything—central line, IV, feeding tube, catheter."

"Get her down to x-ray and get an MRI now," snapped the charge nurse. "Mrs. Durano, we're not sure what happened here, but we're going to take care of Amberle. Go to the waiting area. We'll give you an update as soon as we can."

"Don't go, Mom," Amberle begged.

"Your mom can come back later," the nurse promised. "Right now, we need to clean you up. Please go, Mrs. Durano, so we can take care of your daughter."

Everything in me screamed no, but my voice didn't come. I felt tears on my cheeks as I struggled to my feet. "I'll be back, Amberle. Very soon. I love you."

Amberle's sobs were replaced by my own as I walked down the hallway to the waiting room. It was empty and dark. Like me.

Chapter Eight

Why?

I closed my eyes to pray but fell asleep.

"Mrs. Durano?" I forced myself into alertness. "You can see Amberle now."

I hurried to Amberle's room. The floor was clean, and Amberle's new, white dressings belied the calamity two hours earlier.

"Sweetie, what happened?"

"It just seemed so real," she said as she described the horrifying house fire in her dream. "Eva's family was trapped, and they were all suffocating. The adults started leaping out the windows, but Eva was scared and wouldn't go. She was the only one who didn't have a choice—because she didn't know what to do. I knew I could save her if I jumped out of my skin and we escaped together. So, I did." Amberle's words were filled with emotion, as if she didn't know whether the dream was true.

"So, you saved her?" I asked, trying to understand her hallucination.

"Uh-huh. She's OK now." Amberle seemed genuinely relieved. Her breathing slowed.

"And how are you?"

"I'm OK too. Can't you tell?"

I kissed Amberle's forehead and stroked her hair until she fell asleep. The charge nurse came in to check her vitals.

"What in the world happened?" I asked, not knowing whether to be angry the accident occurred or relieved Amberle was OK.

"Somehow, your daughter found the strength to jump out of bed. Don't ask me how. She lost her IV, central line, catheter, everything. We replaced it all and gave her wound care. She did lose some blood but didn't break anything except the bedrail. I'm afraid, Mrs. Durano, we may need to restrain her at night." She reached into her pocket, pulled out two canvas straps, and moved toward the bed.

"Wait. Please, instead of doing that, tonight, can I just sleep here? Please?"

"We can't have this happen again."

"I know. It won't. Just bring me a pillow and a blanket. I'll sleep right here. I won't let anything happen. I promise." I searched her eyes for sympathy. "Please, can we talk about the restraints in the morning?"

The nurse nodded and left the room. Later, she returned with a pillow and blanket.

As I settled into my makeshift bed, I thought of Amberle rescuing Eva from the fire. Perhaps it was more of a vision than a dream. Not a housefire, but an eternal fire. Amberle had knitted her heart to this precious child and recently asked Eva if she could teach her how to pray. Eva had agreed. Even in her weakened, drug-induced state, Amberle managed to love God and love others, to find purpose in both her life and her dreams.

I could not. My purpose was to find answers, and, at that moment, I had none. I mistakenly believed my peace and purpose were dependent on knowing why instead of recognizing I already had the answer in my relationship with God

Amberle groaned loudly. I sat up and put one hand on her shoulder and another on her leg. Her head and arms thrashed wildly, and her mouth moved, trying to form words.

"What is it, honey? What is it?"

"It's a night terror," said the nurse, who rushed in when she heard the noise. "Fourth night in a row." She pressed a button on the machine that controlled the dosage of Amberle's pain medication. "That should calm her down."

†

It was barely 6:00 a.m. when the doctor came to check on Amberle. I was startled when she switched on the lights. Amberle continued to sleep.

"I heard she had a rough night." The doctor inspected Amberle's new bandages, wrote something on a notepad, and disappeared as quickly as she'd come in.

Although visitors' restrictions had officially been lifted, Amberle was too exhausted to see anyone that morning. She shivered uncontrollably, and the nurses worked hard to stabilize her. Sometimes, they let me stay in her room; other times, they didn't.

Word about last night's accident spread, and Amberle's Facebook page exploded with prayers and well wishes.

When I saw Amberle that afternoon, she seemed better. "Last night, you had a nightmare. Do you remember it?"

"You mean the one about the fire?"

"No. I think you had another one, too. A different one. Do you remember?"

"Oh, the one about the hooded guy in the shadows. He's been coming here a lot lately. He wants me to eat cat food, but I always say no."

"Cat food?" I asked.

Kelly heard us and entered the room. "Excuse me . . . those nightmares, I think we've come up with an idea that might help."

"That would be great," I said.

"Amberle, you've been having a lot of night terrors lately. We think you're experiencing something similar to sundowner syndrome. Do you know what that is?"

I could see Amberle reaching into her mental files. "It's a temporary dementia, common in Alzheimer's patients and people who are sleep deprived."

"Exactly," Kelly replied. "I checked your med schedule, and since you've been in the Burn ICU, we've been waking you every two hours at night to give you eye drops to prevent corneal scratching. You're not getting enough deep sleep. And with all the people who love you and come to visit every day, you're not able to take naps either. So, I suggested to the docs that you get at least six hours of uninterrupted sleep each night. That might help get rid of those hallucinations and night terrors."

"That'd be great," I said. "But what about her eye medication?"

"We'll watch it. Maybe the night nurse can give her a stronger dose right before bed. Anyway, right now, rest is really important."

"So, no restraints?" I asked.

Kelly smiled. "No restraints."

Later that afternoon, Kelly poked her head in the door. "Amberle?" She smiled. "You have a visitor—Chancellor Boschini."

"V-Bo!" Amberle shouted. That was the students' nickname for the man who steered Texas Christian University. As one of TCU's sixty-five chancellor scholars, Amberle knew Victor Boschini. They spoke as if they were old friends. I felt awkward, but his warmth and sincerity soon put me at ease.

After about twenty minutes, he turned to leave. "Hey, you better get well soon. We miss you, Amberle. TCU's not the same without you."

I was glad to see Dr. Hawley and another professor, Dr. Susan Weeks, at the four o'clock visiting time. While other friends chatted with Amberle, I pulled her professors aside.

"What do you think of the change in the medication schedule?" I asked.

They agreed Amberle's mental state needed to be the top concern.

The alarm on my watch went off. It was time to leave for the airport. I dreaded Tuesday evenings because that was when I had to leave Dallas to return to Albuquerque. Every Wednesday, I directed children's choir at Calvary Chapel, and on Thursdays, I did college advising for high school juniors and seniors. I loved my work. It was a healthy distraction. But in Albuquerque, I was on autopilot. My body was there, but my mind and heart were in Dallas.

I squeezed through Amberle's cadre of friends to kiss her goodbye. "I love you bunches. I'll see you Friday morning. Sleep well. I mean it."

"I love you too," she said.

"I'll keep you posted," Diane promised.

"We've got her, Mama D," Lyndsey added. "Have a good flight."

The lights of Dallas dimmed as I headed to Albuquerque. I stared into the darkness. *How much more, Lord?*

I knew the first words out of everyone's mouth in Albuquerque would be "How is she?" *How would I respond?*

Regardless of my answer, words of encouragement would follow: "Don't worry. God won't give you more than you can handle. Trust Him."

God won't give you more than you can handle. Over the last few days, several friends had encouraged me with that promise from First Corinthians, but right now, I didn't believe it. *Really, Lord?* I opened my Bible app. There it was—chapter ten, verse thirteen: "God is faithful; he will not let you be tempted beyond what you can bear. But when you are tempted, he will also provide a way out so that you can endure it" (1 Corinthians 10:13 NIV).

Wait. What did it say? I read the verse again.

That verse said nothing about a *situation* being too difficult to handle. That verse was about overwhelming temptation. Yes, I'd been tempted to doubt God, and I'd succumbed to it. But I also knew the way out: to focus on what I knew instead of what I didn't. I was just trying to handle a living hell. Alone.

Then it came to me. That was the temptation—to handle it myself. Yet God promised a way out.

Although I didn't quite understand it, I knew the way out didn't mean finding an answer. It meant learning to trust God. Completely.

Chapter Nine

The Word

As expected, everyone wanted to know about Amberle's progress. They assumed after nearly two weeks in the hospital, she would be better.

I knew, regardless of what I told them, they would hear what they wanted to hear. I understood that, so I told them, "She's still having problems, but God is faithful."

But God. Two words that made the difference between life and death. Hope and despair. Circumstance and Truth. I wanted to believe my words, but I wasn't sure they were true. I wanted to shout, "Life sucks, and I don't know if I can trust God right now." But I wasn't ready to give up.

†

When I returned to Dallas on Friday afternoon, Kelly gave me the news: Amberle's condition had peaked. She was on the road to recovery.

I wanted to do a happy dance, but something about Kelly's demeanor told me I shouldn't.

"This is going to be the hardest part," she warned. "When Amberle was on the uphill side of this battle, we allowed her to rest, to use all her energy toward getting better. Now she's going to have to work. She has to learn how to sit, stand, walk, eat, go to the bathroom—everything you and I take for granted. It's not going to be easy. A lot of times it's one step forward and two steps back. But I know Amberle can do it. In fact, yesterday, she sat up in bed for about three minutes. You would have been so proud. We're going to try to get her to stand today."

"Really?" I didn't know whether to be concerned or excited. "Are you sure she's ready?"

Kelly smiled. "If we wait until she's ready, it'll never happen."

I took Kelly's words to heart and prayed we would be brave.

Later that afternoon, four nurses and a physical therapist guided Amberle through the mechanics of standing up. It was exhausting to watch and took every ounce of Amberle's energy. When her feet finally touched the floor and the nurses let go, Amberle balanced for about thirty seconds. We cheered as if she'd completed a triathlon.

The next day, Amberle's body revolted. Her temperature spiked to 103 degrees, and her heart rate exceeded 140. I texted her friends and asked them not to come. Amberle needed to rest.

Midmorning, a nurse I didn't recognize glided into Amberle's room. "Dr. Arnoldo said this might help." She held up a shot with a long needle.

"Is that one of those stomach injections?" Amberle moaned.

I stood up. "Amberle doesn't feel well right now. I know you're just following doctor's orders, but she's already in enough pain . . ."

"Mom," Amberle interrupted. "It's OK."

I tried to speak again, but Amberle motioned for me to sit down.

Amberle cried when the nurse gave her the shot and apologized immediately. "I'm sorry," she said, gulping down tears. "It just hurts so much."

I felt useless trying to defend my daughter.

After the nurse left the room, Amberle turned to me. "Mom, don't ever do that again. These people need to see the love of Christ. I don't care how you feel, and I don't care how I feel. We need to show the love of Jesus. In everything."

I wanted to defend myself, but I knew she was right. Her words were true. "Do you want me to apologize to the nurse?"

"No," Amberle said. "It's too late for that. Just don't let it happen again."

†

Although I'd promised to remain positive and trust God every step of the way, I found myself waffling. Sitting in Amberle's room, watching her sleep gave me time to both worry and work.

I knew the doctors said Amberle was improving, but I couldn't see it. From the top of her head down to her ankles, she was covered with black scabs and silver-colored scar tissue. Her internal organs were still sloughing because she coughed in fits every time a piece of the lining of her trachea or lungs interfered with her breathing. She had a thin, red film on her teeth and frequently asked for a tissue so she could spit out blood-filled saliva.

I stared at her war-torn body. *Lord, what if she never sees again? What if she doesn't graduate? What if she never becomes a nurse?*

I felt guilty for asking questions, but they were real. I wasn't asking questions to challenge Him. I just wanted to understand. I didn't yet realize that God doesn't require understanding; He just requires obedience, which is a result of love (John 14:15). And the highest form of obedience is trust. How different my perspective would have been if my questions had come from a desire for intimacy rather than a craving for independence.

I closed my eyes to escape.

Look at her, I sensed God say. *Look at her feet.*

What?

Hesitant to believe what had just happened and, even more, to believe Whose voice I'd heard, I opened my eyes and glanced around the room. My eyes settled on Amberle's feet. They were the only part of her body that was unscathed, without a single blister or blemish.

"Read Isaiah 52:7."

What?

"Isaiah 52:7."

I reached for my Bible and turned to a familiar verse. It was familiar because I'd heard the words hundreds of times, but I'd never known the citation. I was lazy that way. "How beautiful on the mountains are the feet of those who bring the good news . . ." (NIV).

My unbelief turned to wonder as I read the words again; this time, aloud: "How beautiful on the mountains are the *feet* of those who bring the good news . . . " (NIV, emphasis added).

My eyes fixed on the page as I realized what had just occurred. I looked at Amberle's feet, then back to the words on the page. Amberle's feet *were* beautiful, miraculously untouched by her catastrophic condition. And absolutely beautiful.

Did He just do that? Did God just . . .?

Questions flooded my mind, and, for once, I didn't care. Even though I didn't know the answer, I knew that Voice.

God was here. At the hospital and at home. His power and His peace were mine in His Word.

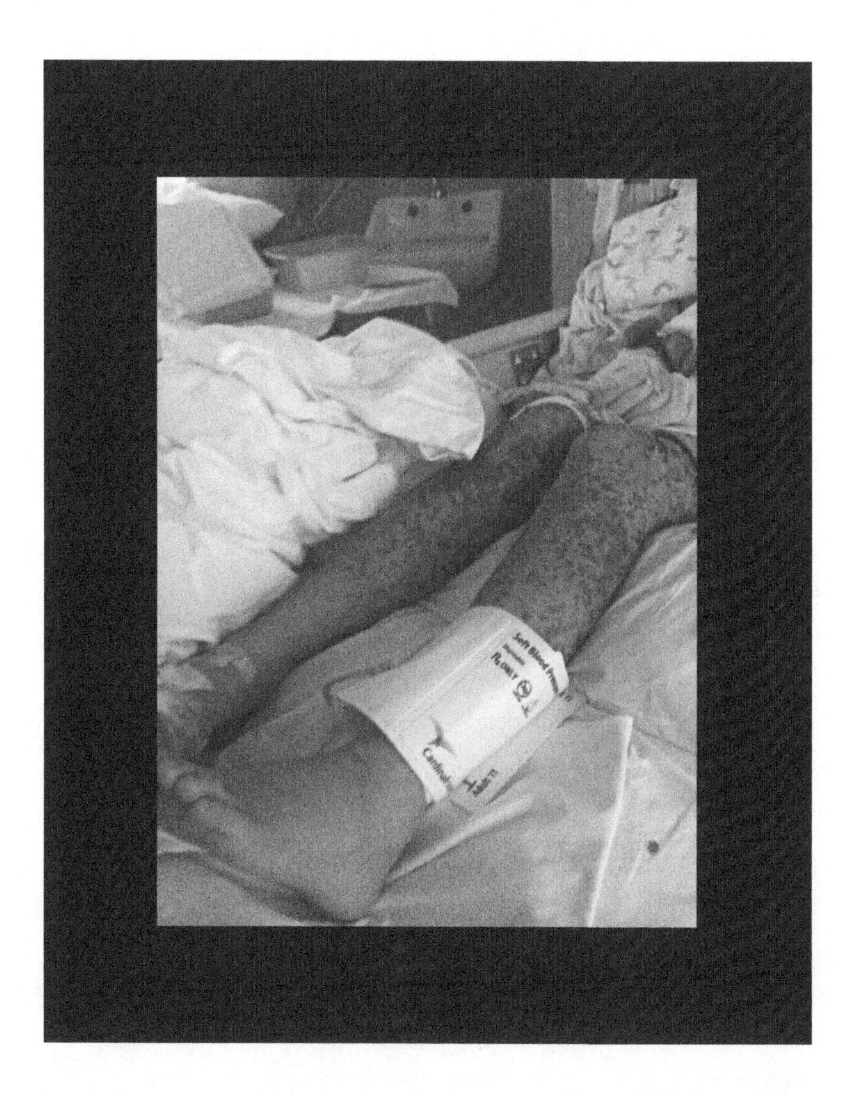

Sure, I'd been reading the Bible daily, but now He'd spoken to me—specifically and intimately. I needed this miracle, and He'd given it to me through His Word.

Although I had no idea how it was going to happen, at that moment, I knew, one day, God would use Amberle to bring His gospel to the world.

But first, she had to get well.

†

Amberle worked hard the next few days. Progress was slow. I was glad when she felt well enough for visits from friends, especially when I had to return to Albuquerque on Tuesday evening.

When I returned to Dallas two days later and walked into Amberle's room, she was sitting in a chair, surrounded by nurses. She looked like a princess with her ladies-in-waiting. Except she was crying.

"I'm sorry. I'm sorry," she repeated.

"Shh, honey. You have nothing to be sorry for," said one of the nurses. "We know this is painful."

I craned my neck to see what was happening. Each nurse was removing small pieces of dead, black skin from her face. As they carefully plucked the tiny scabs from her forehead, cheeks, and chin, new, red-tinted, baby-soft skin appeared.

After several minutes, Kelly stopped the process. "I think that's enough for today. You're a brave girl, Amberle. It's a heck of a way to get a facial, huh?"

Amberle smiled weakly. "A full-body facial, you mean."

The nurses laughed, and I saw their genuine compassion. "It's hard, honey, but you are getting better. Your body is working the way it's supposed to. Keep this up, and you'll be moving to Acute Care by the end of the month."

"What?" I asked.

"Acute Care," the nurse said. "It's the next level down. The docs evaluate each patient at the end of the month. If a patient's strong enough, we move her."

"Really?" My heart wanted to explode with hope, but my previous disappointments stopped me.

The nurses left the room.

Amberle and I sat quietly for a few minutes, and then Amberle began to cry. “Oh, honey, what is it? What’s wrong?”

“I—I don’t know if I can keep this up, Mom,” she stuttered between sobs, “and I don’t want to disappoint you.”

I hugged Amberle tightly. Her words were difficult, but they were real, and I needed to hear her. She was emotionally and physically exhausted.

I was too, and I wanted to honor Amberle’s honesty with an honest response. But somehow, I couldn’t come up with a word.

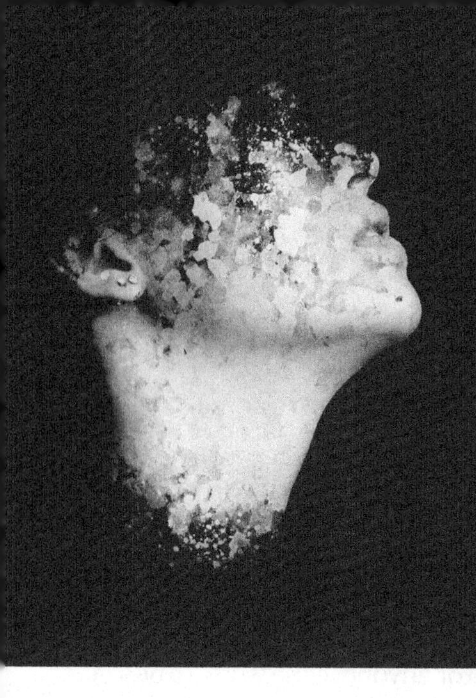

Chapter Ten

Armed and Dangerous

Two steps forward, one step back. Mentally. Spiritually. Emotionally. I prayed this would not be the case physically. Because I idolized answers, I brought much of the instability on myself. Sometimes I recognized my misdirected desires, but all too often, I found myself longing more for clarity than for Christ.

Now that Amberle's TEN had peaked, her skin was deteriorating rapidly. Nurses told me it was part of the healing process, although it certainly didn't look that way. Multiple blisters popped every day, exposing not only gaping wounds underneath but also my deepest fears.

Writing relieved some stress and helped me process what was happening. The *Caring Bridge* blog connected me to the outside world and forced me to stay positive since I focused on our family's faith. I didn't have time to look at readers' comments on the blog. I regret I didn't make that more of a priority—but when I did, their words warmed my heart.

I never understood why people responded to the blog with such empathy. My writing was raw and unfiltered. Perhaps that was what drew people to the site. In a world saturated with superficiality, people ache for transparency. Everyone hurts, but no one cries. We're all afraid, but no one asks for help. We think it's a sin or shows a lack of faith if anyone admits fear, pain, or uncertainty—to see ourselves as we really are. The way God sees us. And loves us anyway.

But doubt, fear, and pain are not sinful. They are weaknesses, commonalities with the rest of mankind. Fortunately, most of my readers knew that; they identified with me and promised to pray. Except for one: Jesus.

Yep, Jesus Christ told me I was doing it all wrong. At least, that's who "signed" the comment left on *Caring Bridge*.

"Dear Amberle, You are healed. The reason you have not seen your healing is because you haven't received it by faith. That's all you have to do. Just believe. It is not my will for you or anyone in the world to be sick. Sickness does not glorify me. You are only sick because of your lack of faith. Believe, my child, and you will be healed. I love you always, Jesus."

Hmmm.

God was fully capable of healing Amberle. I knew that. Now, a sentiment I vaguely detected in some of our friends' sympathies was right there in black and white. Was our lack of faith preventing Amberle's healing?

I had my share of Pentecostal experiences. I worked for the Christian Broadcasting Network and attended an Assemblies of God church for years. I believe in the moving of the gifts of the Holy Spirit, and I speak in tongues, but I never subscribed to the idea that God will *always* heal if you have enough faith. God can heal, and He does heal. But I don't believe He *has* to.

Putting faith in *my* faith to change a circumstance didn't make sense to me. But maybe I didn't get it. More than changing my situation, I felt God needed to change me. I thought about the apostles. They had some pretty horrible circumstances, and yet, many times, God didn't change their situation. Instead, He helped them through it.

Sure, I would've loved God to deliver us wholly and immediately, but I had a sense we would see God more in the journey than in the destination. I was starting to discover the truth that God's love isn't primarily demonstrated by our situation; it's demonstrated by our relationship.

However, I couldn't see that truth until I admitted my helplessness. I wrestled with God daily, accusing Him of abandonment, and although the fight was futile, it was far from worthless. I knew who would win in the end—and it wasn't me. Still, I continued to wrestle because it kept me in close contact with Christ. Ultimately, wrestling with God was better than sitting in uncertainty because I discovered that when God wins, I win too. However, my win had to come through surrender.

Sitting in the black leather recliner in Amberle's hospital room, I wondered why, if I was surrendered to God, did I still feel like I was in a war zone? I knew Ephesians 6 had a lot to say about spiritual warfare and "the armor of God," so I turned to the scripture for guidance. As I read through the familiar words, my eyes settled on verse 17 (NIV): "Take the helmet of salvation and the sword of the Spirit, which is the word of God." From previous teachings, I knew God's Word, Scripture, was the only offensive weapon in the bunch. All the other pieces of armor—the belt of truth, breastplate of righteousness, sandals of peace, shield of faith, and helmet of salvation—were defensive.

In my mind, I saw a strange image—a Roman soldier dressed in battle gear, kneeling, reading His Bible, with his sheathed sword by his side. The soldier was being bombarded by enemy fire. He wasn't dead, but he wasn't defending himself either. *Why is he just kneeling there, reading? Why doesn't he get up and fight?*

I remembered a sermon on spiritual warfare. The speaker told believers that in order to wield the sword of the Spirit and defeat Satan, they had to say God's Word aloud. Satan isn't omniscient, he said, so in order for the enemy to feel the power of God's Word, our sword, you have to say it aloud.

OK. It can't hurt.

I glanced towards the open door of Amberle's hospital room. Nurses in blue scrubs sat at their stations, focused on their work.

Amberle was asleep, and the room was silent except for the beeping of her monitors.

I read the words before me aloud, quietly at first: "Finally, be strong in the Lord and in his mighty power." As I made my way from Ephesians 6:10 through verse twenty, I became louder. More confident. Then, I stopped.

Was I imagining it or did I actually feel better? Less afraid?

I remembered a familiar verse: "So then faith comes by hearing, and hearing by the word of God" (Romans 10:17 NKJV).

My faith did feel stronger after hearing my voice read Scripture aloud.

I thought about how people react differently to the same circumstance. The doctors were motivated by the situation and searched for a way to help. I was afraid because I didn't know how I could help. But now I did.

They could fight the physical battle, and I would fight the spiritual one. Two equally intense campaigns with one critical difference.

In the physical realm, Amberle's life was in danger. The risk was real, and the result, uncertain. In the spiritual battle, victory was assured when I used God's Word to "demolish strongholds" and "take captive every thought" (2 Corinthians 10:4–5 NIV).

Spiritual success didn't mean the situation would change, but it did mean I could fight my fears and find my peace. I identified the lies I believed and confronted the foundations of my fears—lies about not being loved and not being heard by God, about earning God's favor through my behavior, and about how God's love means living a life of ease. All deceptions of the enemy.

Every fear is learned, and every fear is based on a lie. That's why Scripture says "perfect love drives out fear" (1 John 4:18 NIV). I knew God's love in my head, but the lies of the enemy had stolen it from my heart.

Forgive me, Lord, for believing Satan's lies. Help me to see Your truth.

That prayer was my first step toward victory—identifying the lies of the enemy and recognizing the Truth of God's Love.

Yes, the spiritual battle we were fighting was just as real as the physical one, but with one enormous difference. The spiritual battle—the fear—was the result of my *thinking*; I believed lies that weren't true. Therefore, the fear was only a threat, not an actual danger—because I could control my thinking by applying God's Word—and that's exactly what Satan didn't want me to know. I couldn't control the circumstance, but I *could* control my reaction to it by believing God's Word. I couldn't change the situation or the difficulty of it, but I could allow *it* to change me.

Now, I was armed and dangerous. With God's Word.

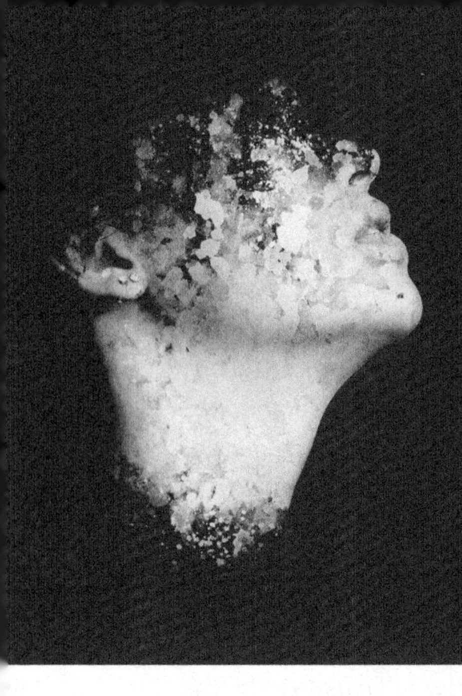

Chapter Eleven

Crazy

From Dallas to Albuquerque and back again. That was my routine, but there was nothing routine about it. I survived on autopilot, doing what needed to be done without any awareness of my own consciousness.

Not Amberle.

Bombarded by physicians and curious interns who studied her as if she were a sideshow attraction, Amberle was constantly reminded of her situation. Who she was, who she wasn't, and who she might never be.

Amberle's desire for normalcy made her ask hard questions of her healthcare providers. Questions I never would have asked—for fear of the answer or the lack of one. She reprimanded them for sugar-coating their responses and demanded integrity. Her prognosis was grim: months of recovery, chronic health problems, continuing pain, and possible blindness.

The facts wore her down, and Amberle began to retreat. Friends still visited, but conversations became sparse. She pretended to sleep while they were in the room because she couldn't face her own reality. Fortunately, Amberle's friends realized their presence was the greatest gift they could give, with or without dialogue, so they continued to visit.

Their unselfish love aided Amberle's recovery more than they knew. Weeks later, in her journal, Amberle wrote:

> *There were days when I'm sure that the Bible passage that a nurse read me in the morning or the fervent prayer at my bedside was far more important than any other treatment. Little things like holding someone's hand. I know there were countless treatments I wouldn't have endured without that hand squeeze, whether from a close friend or a stranger nursing student. Despite the difficulties of being in the hospital for thirty-five days, I have some wonderfully sweet memories, thanks to my community of friends that enveloped me so tightly in their loving care and prayers. When I was finally able to see, I realized that every inch of my wall was covered with cards from people near and far, filled with encouraging words and heartfelt prayers . . . One morning I awoke to find that Cheraya had come early that morning simply to watch me sleep. Chelsea and Mathilde, whom I didn't even know before I was admitted to Parkland, would do the same after they got off their twelve-hour nursing shifts here. It was so moving to me that these precious sisters cared not about spending time with me that would reward them or be exceedingly enjoyable but simply that they wanted to sacrifice their time at my bedside. I remember being especially thankful after Lyndsey left one day, knowing that the quality time I got to spend with her in that hospital room was something I could have gotten nowhere else. A hand squeeze in the ICU, a chapter of Isaiah, help with my bath . . . all these moments have become precious memories to me, highlighting the incredible character of the friends that I am so blessed to have.*

Amberle had hundreds of burden-bearers (Galatians 6:2), and without a doubt, they pulled her through these darkest of days. Looking back, if I'd known the power of the ministry of presence, I might have asked Christina to return to Dallas. But I didn't. Professional caregivers tended to Amberle's body while personal caregivers healed Amberle's soul.

Dr. Hawley noticed Amberle's downward spiral and pulled Kelly and me aside. "We need to accelerate her recovery before depression sets in. Give her a challenge."

"Great idea," Kelly said. "I'll check with the docs and see what we can do."

The next day, a cadre of therapists and nurses descended on Amberle's room. "Today, you start walking," Kelly announced.

After half an hour of reminding Amberle of the things her mind knew but her body had forgotten, Amberle walked. Two nurses held her on each side, and one followed in case she collapsed. Amberle shuffled one foot in front of the other twenty feet down the hall, encouraged by a combination of coaxing and cheering from the hospital staff. Afterward, she collapsed in the chair in her room.

"I did it, Mom; I did it," Amberle heaved.

"You sure did. That's a big deal." What some might have labeled a small step on the path to recovery was a total conquest to us.

Later that day, Amberle received more good news. "Your skin is looking better," said Dr. Liesel, Amberle's dermatologist. "Your back's still raw because you've been lying down so much, so you need to sit up when you can. We'll keep you moisturized to minimize the scarring. It should take about three weeks for your skin to completely regenerate. Stay strong and keep up the good work."

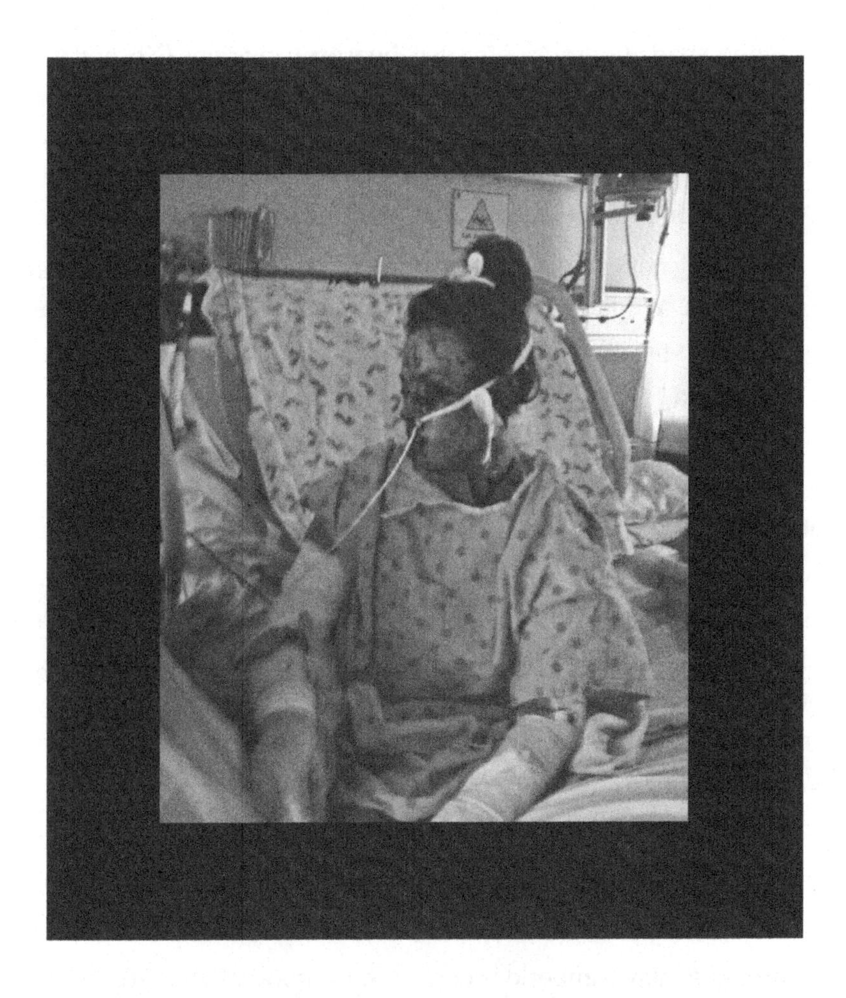

"I'll try." After Dr. Liesel left the room, Amberle turned to me. A single tear rolled down her cheek. "They talk like it's all up to me, but I don't know what else I can do."

I leaned over and held her hand. "You're doing everything you can, and we're all very proud of you."

"But is that enough, Mom? I'm tired. I don't want to do this anymore."

This. This stranglehold. This annihilation. This hell.

As we sat in silence, I asked God what I could do. I was desperate for something, anything related to hope.

"Mom, can you read a little of the Bible to me? It always makes me feel better. How about the book of John?" Amberle knew where hope lived.

I opened my Bible and read the familiar words, "In the beginning was the Word, and the Word was with God, and the Word was God . . ." (John 1:1 NKJV). After a few moments, Amberle was asleep.

Thank you, Lord, for Your peace.

I continued reading to myself, searching for that same tranquility. I came to verse 14: "And the Word became flesh and dwelt among us."

Flesh? The word arrested me.

I read it again. "And the Word became . . ."

"Flesh," I said aloud. That was the miracle we wanted. The healing she needed. Was this the answer?

Lord, are you saying . . .? I thought about it for a moment and decided I was reading too much into the verse. But the thought wouldn't leave. I knew that verse referred to Christ's incarnation, but could it mean something else too? I didn't want to manipulate Scripture for my purpose—as if I could make Amberle's flesh grow by using God's Word as a talisman.

Not more than a week before that, however, God had reminded me of the power of Scripture and encouraged me to use His Word as a weapon against fear. Didn't Isaiah 55:11 promise His Word accomplishes what He desires? I didn't understand it. At all.

A thought quickly came to mind, and I dismissed it. *No, that's crazy. Nuts.*

Nevertheless, that night, I found myself with a large poster board in front of me and a thick, black marker in my hand. Carefully, I penned, "AND THE WORD BECAME FLESH . . ." Underneath, in smaller letters, I wrote an explanation: "We believe in the power of God's Word. If you believe it too, please encourage Amberle by writing your favorite Scripture below and signing your name." Then I wrote Isaiah 55:10–11 (NIV): "As the rain and the snow come down from heaven, and do not return to it without watering the earth and making it bud and flourish, so that it yields seed for the sower and bread for the eater, so is my word that goes out from my mouth: It will not return to me empty, but will accomplish what I desire and achieve the purpose for which I sent it."

The next morning, I hung the poster on Amberle's door. By midday, several people had written Scriptures on it. When visiting hours finished, the poster had nearly a dozen verses on it.

It wasn't that I believed Scripture held some sort of magical spell; God is the Great Physician—and I had to constantly re-place my faith in Him, not in what He does. But I couldn't shake the thought that God created the universe simply by speaking (Genesis 1:1–1:27) or the belief that His Word is living and active (Hebrews 4:12). As the number of Scriptures written on the poster grew, it became obvious that others believed those truths as well. I didn't know if my small act of faith would ultimately change the situation, but I knew it would change me.

Before I flew back to Albuquerque, the poster was completely full. I recognized quite a few of her friends' names, but nurses, therapists, and physicians had signed the poster too.

After I returned to Dallas, Kelly pulled me aside. "I never knew so many of us were Christians. Everybody who works here is compassionate and capable, but we never talked about our faith. Now, we do, and it's great. Thanks for bringing faith out into the open."

I smiled. *I guess it wasn't such a crazy idea after all.*

Chapter Twelve

In Dependence

Recovery. It's a happy word . . . or at least, that's what I thought. Recovery is supposed to be a time of ease and flowers, naps, and comfy pillows. But as I discover daily, recovery is much easier said than done. Maybe it's because I don't remember the raw horror of my actual decline, but I have found, more often than not, recovery is two steps forward and three backward. I grow so tired so quickly, and it takes conscious effort to want to continue putting in the effort and energy to get better.

As a recovering patient, I kind of envisioned everything just disappearing or disintegrating into happy wellness, but reality is showing me that a lot of this downhill slope is about endurance for the extended time of recovery.

As a worsening patient, I didn't have to do that much or wonder what to expect the next day, getting my hopes up all too often. I do continue to climb this sometimes seemingly insurmountable obstacle, but as the Lord reminds me again and again, He is faithful. I'm thankful I don't really seem to "understand the gravity" of the situation, generally being assured that everything will be fine no matter what. It seems the recovery period will last about a year in full, but in reality, TEN will be something I never fully leave. It is a part of my past, a contour in my sculpture. I used to wonder why I had never been in a trial or suffered persecution, but I kind of had a hunch God was sparing me pain because I would have my full share at some later point. In my mind, this point was my martyrdom as a missionary. But, as almost-a-missionary from the hospital bed, I think maybe it was for this. I never really had those dark times most people highlight in their testimonies . . . Perhaps this is my "for such a time as this" (Esther 4:14).

†

Step by tiny glorious step, Amberle became stronger each day. She learned how to walk, lift a utensil to her mouth, and brush her hair again. Her body didn't always follow her brain, but it wasn't for lack of trying.

Sometimes, Amberle lost patience with herself. It was easy to look at the end goal and get overwhelmed, discounting the daily progress of standing two minutes longer than the day before and lifting her arm another ten degrees. We wanted to move in milestones rather than minutes, but we took what we could get. Amberle knew her recovery wasn't based merely on what she wanted; if that was the case, it would've happened long ago. Amberle's progress was shaped by what she willed herself to do, in spite of her exhaustion and anguish.

That indomitable stubbornness paid off when Amberle was moved to the Acute Care Unit on October 30, 2012. Families of the other patients said it would be a callous transition. The nurses said it would foster independence. Instead of having a one-to-one nurse-to-patient ratio like the Burn ICU did, the Acute Care Unit had one-to-five.

I taped Amberle's get-well cards to the wall and put up her few belongings in her new room while we waited for a nurse to come and introduce herself. No one came. After a while, I asked Amberle, "Isn't it time for your meds?"

I pressed the call button. After twenty minutes, a middle-aged nurse hurried into the room and handed Amberle her pills. "You can fill the water pitcher in the bathroom," she said.

Before the nurse rushed out, Amberle asked, "Could I please have some moisturizer? My skin's feeling a little tight." It was a common complaint now that Amberle's skin was regenerating.

The woman left and returned in a few moments. "Here." She tossed Amberle a tube of cream. "Put it on yourself."

Amberle and I looked at each other. "I guess this is what they call independence," she said.

I felt a little like the Israelites in Exodus, wanting to turn back to a more difficult time (in the ICU), simply because it was familiar (Numbers 14:1–4). I reminded myself that even though it was more difficult, Acute Care was a better place to be because Acute Care was on the way out.

When Amberle took her pills, she began to gag. In the Burn ICU, Kelly would've been in the room while Amberle took her pills and would've suctioned Amberle's throat if she gagged. Here, no one came. Amberle's choking became worse. I ran into the hall.

"The suction's on the left side of her bed," a nurse said loudly from inside another patient's room. I ran back to Amberle's bedside and reached for the device, mimicking what I'd seen the nurses do so many times.

"I'll do it, mom," Amberle said between coughs. "It's easier."

Well, she is a nurse, and she knows what she needs. I gave her the gadget and apologized. Crisis averted.

Later that afternoon, Amberle's pain increased. I pressed the call button to request additional medication, but no one answered. "Mom, it feels like needles are poking me all over."

I ran to the nurses' station. It was empty. I returned to the room. Amberle's moaning became louder and louder, and I pressed the call button again and again. After what seemed like an hour but was probably only five or ten minutes, a nurse appeared in the doorway. "What do you want?" she asked.

I wanted to tell her exactly what I wanted, but I remembered Amberle's admonition to always be kind. "Pain meds, please," I said, offering my best fake smile.

Although being in the Acute Care Unit had its challenges, it also had benefits.

Having open visiting hours was Amberle's idea of paradise. Anyone could see Amberle anytime, which meant friends who hadn't visited before due to ICU restrictions now could. A childhood friend even drove from Arkansas to ask Amberle to be her maid of honor. Amberle began weaning herself off her medications so she could remember conversations, but as she did, we saw evidence of PTSD.

I camped out in Amberle's hospital room and slept in a convertible chair next to her bed. While it wasn't necessarily comfortable, it was advantageous (and cheap). Amberle fought sleep because she hated the daily re-orientation to her reality, and due to the membranous eye coverings, she couldn't tell if it was daylight or dark. We asked visitors to leave by 10:00 p.m. each evening and eventually retrained Am's circadian rhythm, but no matter how hard we tried, we couldn't retrain her mind. Amberle couldn't recall the last month of being in the hospital. Looking back, it was a blessing in disguise.

Nearly every day, Amberle asked me, "Is this real?"

"Yes, honey. I'm sorry. It is."

"And how long have I been here?"

My response would be followed by a long silence that indicated Amberle was trying to make sense of her incomprehensible situation, struggling to fill a void no solution could satisfy. Only God could. On days when Amberle recognized the futility of her effort, she simply replied, "I don't want to do this anymore."

Amberle remembered certain feelings: comfort as nurses read Scripture to her during non-visitation hours, relief when she woke up from a midday nap surrounded by friends, and sadly, pain. Lots and lots of pain. When I asked her to describe it, she couldn't. Her suffering was beyond words. Feelings without form, sensations without structure.

"I wish I could remember," she sighed. "Then I'd know if this was real."

Although she was walking every day, Amberle still hadn't seen her reflection in a mirror. I knew that day was coming, and I was concerned about how it would affect her. Her face most accurately reflected the last month's journey—perplexing, complicated, and hideous. I asked Amberle if she wanted to see the photos we'd taken nearly every day since she entered the hospital. Perhaps they would provide context.

She agreed.

I set my laptop in front of her, and she scrolled through the pictures. Slowly. All one hundred and sixty-eight of them. Amberle couldn't see clearly, but she could distinguish the devastation she'd endured. She was horrified. "That's not me, is it?"

She had no understanding, even with photos. The situation made no sense because it couldn't. Deep down, Amberle knew the comprehension she craved wasn't a function of the brain; it was a matter of the heart.

Like the rest of us, Amberle couldn't reconcile the truth of Scripture with the reality of her broken body. Sometimes, early in the morning, I woke to Amberle's sobs, "Why, God? Why?" Amberle's despair was a sign she still had hope. She just didn't see it yet.

On other days, she embraced God's mystery as part of the miracle and saw her situation as an opportunity to trust God. "His power is made perfect in weakness, Mom, and God will use this," she said, reminding me of 2 Corinthians 12:9. Her vulnerability was a gift, and her stubborn hope reminded me that although Scripture doesn't always answer our questions, it does reveal the truth.

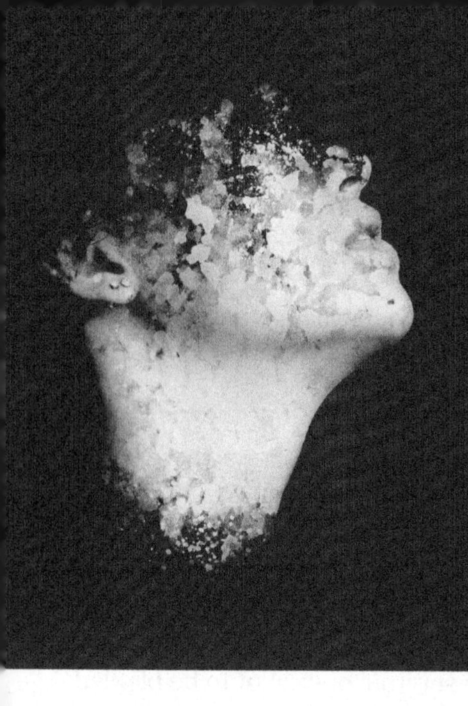

Chapter Thirteen

Hope and Heartache

Visiting "the tank" was Amberle's new adventure—a strange mixture of pain and pleasure. Every other day, Amberle was taken to a room where she was lifted onto a cold steel table. She closed her eyes and focused on her breathing as the med techs removed her bandages. While she covered her private parts with a towel, the techs sprayed her body with soothing warm water and scrubbed away her scabs. Afterward, they wrapped her in warm blankets, and her endorphins soared. According to Amberle, it was a little piece of heaven on earth.

One day, I was invited to join the celebration. As the technicians unwrapped her body, I closed my eyes and squeezed Amberle's hand. When I opened them, I blinked back tears. For the first time, I saw the extent of the damage to Amberle's frame—a sight I could have never imagined. Blood seeped from grey-scabbed wounds and dead skin enveloped her torso like a death shroud. *How is my child still alive?*

"Can you help?" asked one of the med techs.

I didn't want to hurt her.

"The pain is healing, Mom." I took a washcloth and gently cleansed Amberle's shoulders and neck.

"Harder, Mom," she coached.

Amberle knew the pain would ultimately bring healing, just as the removal of the scabs would. So, she endured it, surrendering her pain as part of the process, knowing pain was not the enemy. Pain was the impetus that drew her closer to God. His hope was her help.

As I scrubbed Amberle's back, I thought about the cruelty of the situation. This was not the way things "should be," but the fact that I knew that proved life wouldn't always be this way. Somewhere in my soul, God had placed the knowledge of eternity (Ecclesiastes 3:11), so regardless of how things looked now, I knew Hope was the ultimate reality.

I asked the Lord to scrub the scabs off my heart and empower me to see, not with earthly eyes but with spiritual ones. Not to be blinded by what I saw but empowered by what I knew.

†

As the days went on, Amberle had one question: "When can I leave?"

Like so many answers to our questions before, the reply was always, "We don't know." Until one day in November.

"I think we can start planning for her discharge," Dr. Perumean announced.

My ears heard it, but my mind didn't believe it. "You mean we can go home?"

"Yes, but that doesn't mean she's well. We're at a point where we can't do anything else for her. We just have to wait and see, so she might as well wait at home. Let's see how she does over the next week or so, and we'll think about releasing her."

I didn't know whether to be excited or afraid. Amberle still suffered from extensive nausea, frequent choking, and insomnia. She couldn't bathe herself, dress her wounds, or manage her medications. She had ringing in her ears and almost no vision. She couldn't even walk the length of a hospital hallway.

"Sharon, our social worker, can go through the discharge criteria with you," he said as he left the room.

When Sharon and I met later that morning, I realized the immensity of not only the tasks ahead but also the decisions to be made. We briefly considered having Amberle stay in Fort Worth so she could continue with her current providers, but that wasn't practical. Amberle would return to Albuquerque where I could manage her medical appointments, in-home therapies, and general care. I had no clue about the inner workings of insurance, and Sharon warned me it was a challenge. Since Dee was retired military, we'd have to navigate two of the most bureaucratic agencies in the world to receive care: the military and the insurance industry.

In order for Amberle's physicians to approve her release, she needed to satisfy certain benchmarks before she could leave: walking two lengths of the hospital hallway, standing independently for five minutes, managing her pain, taking care of basic hygiene, and feeding herself without throwing up.

When we told Dr. Hawley our good news, she responded with unnerving honesty. "I'm happy for you, but this is going to be the hardest part of your recovery, Amberle. The hospital has its criteria, but you also need to have your own. You need specific goals, especially if you want to return to school. Before you can even consider returning to TCU, you have to increase your concentration, build your stamina, and improve your vision."

Amberle absorbed Diane's words. "I'll do whatever it takes."

Other than following doctor's orders, Amberle couldn't do anything to repair her vision. She could, however, take responsibility for rebuilding her body and brain. Dr. Hawley prescribed a daily regimen of walking and weightlifting to increase strength, researching and writing to stimulate Amberle's thoughts, and memorizing Scripture to restore concentration.

Over the next few days, Amberle doubled her rehabilitation efforts. When she didn't meet her goals, I mourned over what she couldn't do instead of celebrating what she could. Who would have thought

Amberle's inability to walk an extra twenty feet would have triggered such despair?

With our lives turned upside down, the disappointing truth sometimes tumbled out in unexpected feelings and words, and I was forced to recognize and repent of the offense I held because of Amberle's condition.

Dee and I had always communicated to our children that their success wasn't based on their abilities; we cared more about who they were than what they did. Still, the underlying message of our parenting style was clear: winning creates worth. Now, I was forced to re-evaluate my definitions of purpose, value, and benefit in light of Amberle's limitations. Viewing her imperfections made me come face-to-face with mine.

This became particularly evident one morning as Amberle was checking her email.

"I didn't get it, Mom."

"Get what?" I asked.

She turned up the volume on her computer and asked Siri® to read an email aloud: "Dear Miss Durano, Thank you for your application for the Marshall Scholarship. While your application was exceptional, the committee felt . . ."

I stopped listening, and a lump in my throat hardened. A tear rolled down my cheek, and I tried to sound unaffected. "I'm sorry, honey."

It was the first time I was unable to control my tears in front of her.

"Is that what you care about, Mom? My accomplishments?" She had an edge of anger in her voice.

"Of course not. I'm just disappointed for you."

"But you haven't cried this whole time."

"Honey, just because you don't see it doesn't mean it didn't happen."

'Just because you don't see it.' Wasn't that the definition of hope? Part of me felt foolish for having hope, and now, because my hope was

fractured, I wept in front of my daughter. I was heartsick that Amberle thought my tears were based on her lack of achievement.

At that moment, my heart revealed the insecurity I'd wrestled with since Amberle entered the hospital. More than tears of sadness, these were tears of frustration. At myself. Looking back over my reactions the last few days, I realized my hope was often in a result or a change of circumstance. I felt ashamed for shouting, "Praise God!" in response to a good report but not having the same attitude for a negative one, when faith was most necessary.

I couldn't control the outcome as to whether Amberle received the Marshall Scholarship, but I needed to control my reaction. To any situation. And a proper reaction was rooted in a proper belief, which I knew I had.

Finding stability in the storm wasn't a matter of determination, having the right attitude, or knowing all the answers. It was a matter of depending on God. And regarding the answers I so diligently sought, I only needed one, although my question took various forms: Does God *really* love me? Does God care? If He does, why doesn't He do something?

I was fed up with theological truths and mental assents. I wanted to *feel* His love, not just *know* it.

Then, like the 1980s *Urban Cowboy* song, it hit me: maybe I was looking for love in all the wrong places. *Wait. No.* I was looking for love in Christ, so that was the right place, but maybe what I was looking for wasn't love, but *proof* of his love: proof I thought could only be found in a positive outcome. Because God's blessings prove His love for His children, right?

Wrong.

God's blessings prove His character, *not* His love.

The relationship God chooses to have with each of us proves His love, and if God never blesses us again, we have to be OK with that.

Because He's already done everything He needed to do. "It is finished" (John 19:30).

This journey wasn't just about healing Amberle. It was about discovering Truth.

†

Hope and heartache found a balance those last days in the hospital. Watching Amberle struggle was hard; sometimes I wanted to lower my expectations, but we both knew the integrity of Amberle's choices determined the quality of her results. The hard choice was not always bad, and the easy choice wasn't always good.

One of Amberle's most difficult decisions had to do with returning to TCU. In the beginning, it seemed like Amberle had options when we spoke to her advisors and professors. Some were willing to give her partial credit for the semester, but others could not. We explored finishing the semester online, but Amberle's recovery required every ounce of her energy. Ultimately, the only reasonable decision was for Amberle to take full medical withdrawal from TCU, and even then, her doctors informed us they weren't comfortable with Amberle returning to school in January. Although we knew Amberle's withdrawal from TCU wasn't a failure, we felt as if our world had collapsed.

On November 14, 2012, Amberle was discharged from Parkland Hospital.

It had been forty days since her first symptoms appeared and thirty-five days since she'd entered the hospital. In Scripture, the number forty represents testing. Jesus was in the wilderness forty days; Moses was on Mount Sinai forty days; and the Genesis flood lasted forty days. Was the duration of Amberle's illness coincidental? I didn't think so.

The nurses gently helped Amberle into the rental car, and I buckled her seat belt. As we pulled away from the hospital, Amberle heaved an audible sigh. "I'm glad we're leaving, Mom. Now I'll be able to tell if this was real."

I wished I could tell Amberle it had all been a dream—a nightmarish hallucination, and that now, it was all over. But we both knew it wasn't. As I drove, I sensed Amberle trying to make sense of the situation, but of course, she couldn't.

The doctors gave Amberle permission to spend one night at her house in Fort Worth before heading home to Albuquerque. Amberle hadn't had the chance to mourn the loss of her abilities, and doctors hoped to ease the transition by allowing her to say goodbye to her life at TCU. Her plans, her dreams, and her health were gone.

While dozens of friends loved on Amberle throughout the afternoon and evening, I packed some of her belongings. We'd decided to continue paying her portion of the rent and leave most of her things in Fort Worth, hoping she might be able to return for the spring semester.

It was a long shot, but we were desperate for even a hint of hope.

The next morning, I picked up Amberle, and we drove to the airport.

"I feel like I'm in the wilderness, Mom. I don't know where I'm going or when I'll get there. The only thing that makes me feel better is knowing Jesus was in the wilderness too. And He was led there by the Holy Spirit."

Amberle's sense of being led into the wilderness resonated with me. So much of New Mexico's desert seemed like a wilderness, and that's where we were headed. Then, God brought to mind the wilderness wanderings of the Israelites in the book of Exodus and how He didn't just lead His people to the desert; He led them through it.

As I thought about the fearlessness in Amberle's soul and the anxiety in mine, a Scripture came to mind: "Behold, I am doing a new thing; now it springs forth, do you not perceive it? I will make a way in the wilderness and rivers in the desert" (Isaiah 43:19 ESV).

Lord, make a way.

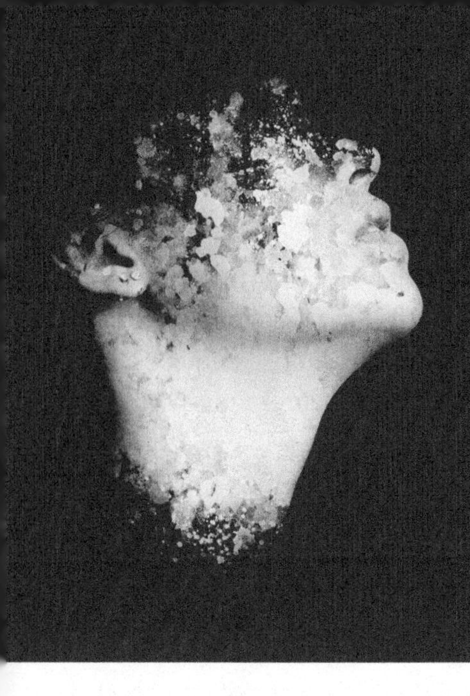

Chapter Fourteen

Perfectly Beautiful

I'm glad you're home," Dee said, giving Amberle a bearhug of love.

"Don't hurt her," I whispered.

"Sorry, sweetie."

Amberle smiled weakly. Dee took the wheelchair from the skycap and tipped him.

"Can you push Amberle out to the car?" I asked. "I'll wait for the luggage, and then you can pick me up. I want to get to the hospital as soon as possible because I don't know how long it will take."

Before Amberle could have a follow-up appointment, we needed to register her in the University of New Mexico Hospital's system. UNMH was the only hospital in Albuquerque with a burn unit. Before we left Parkland, Sharon, the hospital's social worker, had researched providers for Amberle's care in New Mexico. She found an ophthalmologist, internist, audiologist, burn specialist, gastroenterologist, dermatologist, psychiatrist, and a primary care physician who could add other referrals. Normally, pre-scheduling of appointments wasn't allowed, but the doctors were so concerned about Amberle's vision that the schedulers at UNMH's ophthalmology department made an exception. I couldn't wrap my mind around the path that lay before us, but I knew getting Amberle into the system was the first step.

When we arrived at the hospital, we navigated a maze of paperwork in several departments. Each of the medical clerks asked a battery of questions about Amberle's condition. When I answered, sometimes the clerk stopped, looked at Amberle, and replied, "There's not a box for that. I'll make a note."

No, Amberle did not fit in a box. Neither did her condition.

When we finished, I quipped, "That wasn't so bad for the wilderness. Was it, Amberle?"

"No, it really wasn't. Everyone seemed very nice."

It was true. Of course, Amberle couldn't see the pairs of eyes tracking her every move, children pointing and whispering in their mother's ears, wondering "what's wrong with her."

By the time we arrived home, we were exhausted. Our neighbor, Bethany, had decorated Amberle's room with ribbons, balloons, and stuffed animals, and neatly folded on her bed were some comfy new pajamas, a leopard-print robe, and a pink, padded eye shade to block the light that was so painful to her eyes.

I took a few moments to enjoy the lavish love of our neighbor before taking care of the task at hand. "I need to make an appointment with your primary care doc before they close. Just rest."

Amberle's body relaxed in the familiarity of her room.

"Yes, Mrs. Durano. Amberle is in our system. I have her insurance as Tricare Prime. Is that correct?"

"Yes, but I still don't know how insurance works. We've always had our medical care on base. What do I need to do?"

"It's pretty easy," the receptionist explained. "After Dr. McGrew sees Amberle, she'll provide referrals to specialists. Those will be approved by Tricare, and the insurance will take care of the rest."

"That's it?"

"Usually. Do you have any other questions?"

I was sure I did, but I didn't know enough to know what they were.

"We've saved an appointment for Amberle, Monday afternoon at one. Will that work for you?"

"Yes, that's perfect," I replied. "Thank you."

Ending the call, I breathed a prayer of gratitude and laughed to myself. *That's perfect? Perfect would be if I didn't have to make an appointment.* I chided myself for my frustration and recalled some words I'd seen on a kitschy, feel-good sign in some restaurant: "Life doesn't have to be perfect to be beautiful." *Oh, Lord, help me to be satisfied with beautiful, whatever that looks like.* Immediately, one of Amberle's new favorite Scriptures came to mind: "Therefore we do not lose heart. Though outwardly we are wasting away, yet inwardly we are being renewed day by day" (2 Corinthians 4:16 NIV). We were barely home, and already I needed renewal!

I unpacked Amberle's suitcase while she applied several types of eyedrops and tried to take her medications. She gagged and coughed, but finally swallowed the pills. When it was time for dinner, Amberle said she didn't feel like eating. Because her esophagus was so swollen, I knew she wouldn't be able to hold down any of the food our neighbors had provided.

"I'll make you some mashed potatoes. How about that?" I asked.

"Sure. Thanks, Mom. I'm not trying to be difficult."

"I know. Do you want to eat with us, or would you be more comfortable in the bedroom?"

"I want to eat with you. I want to try to be normal."

It would take a long time for life to resemble normal. Getting Amberle ready for bed was a two-hour process and getting her to sleep took even longer. I heard her toss and turn most of the night through the baby monitor we'd installed in her room.

When I walked into the kitchen the next morning, I was shocked to see Amberle, wrapped in a down comforter, her eyes covered by her new pink eye shades, sitting on our back porch.

"What are you doing? It's cold out here."

"I'm watching the sunrise."

"Really?"

"Well, I can't see it, but I can feel it. And it's wonderful. It's good to be home."

I looked at the shimmering rays peeking over the mountains. The trees in our yard held their last vestige of gold and orange, and the sky was sapphire blue. How many mornings had I taken this sight for granted?

Amberle wasn't able to see dawn's splendor with her eyes, but she could sense it in her heart. Seeing her serenity, I wondered how many times I'd missed something wonderful—not because it wasn't there but because I was looking with my eyes instead of my heart.

Perhaps that's why Amberle seemed at peace. She was searching for beauty instead of perfection.

Home in Albuquerque

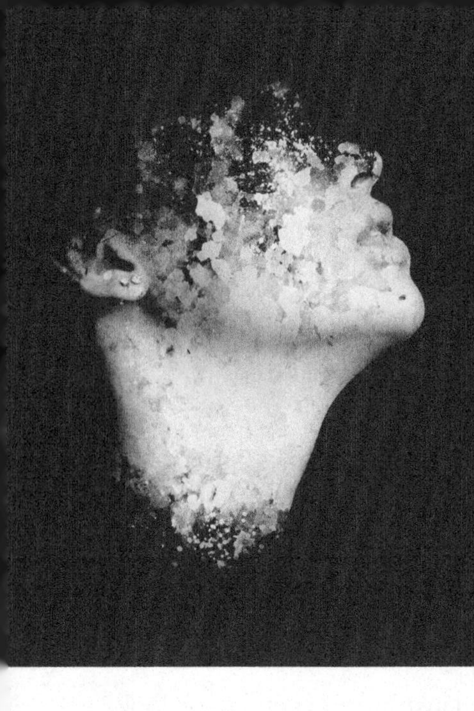

Chapter Fifteen

Helpless

Amberle was able to swallow the oatmeal I prepared for breakfast without much trouble. By the time I gave her all the medications, cleaned the blood from her wounds, lathered her with lotion, and got her dressed, it was noon. I tried not to appear stressed. She was doing her best, and so was I.

As I pushed Amberle through the hospital's hallways, we received quite a few stares, but Amberle didn't notice.

"I'll be strong enough to walk soon," she said.

"Yes, you will, because this afternoon, you start your physical rehab."

We found our way to the corneal specialty unit of the hospital's ophthalmology department, left her wheelchair in the hall, and after checking in, waited in an examination room. I had just helped Amberle into the black leather exam chair when a tall, statuesque woman entered.

"I'm Dr. Rose," she said, shaking our hands. "Let's see what we have here." Amberle squeezed my hand and winced as Dr. Rose shone a spotlight into Amberle's eyes. "TEN, right?"

"Yes, ma'am."

"Hmmm." The doctor reached into a drawer and pulled out a small bottle of what would later become known as "magic golden drops" and a torturous metal device we would grow to hate called a speculum. "I need to get a better look," she said, "but I'm going to put some numbing drops in your eyes first, so it doesn't hurt as much."

She quickly applied the drops. "Now, open your eyes. Wider, please."

Amberle tried to lift her eyelids so the doctor could study her cornea, but it was too painful.

"I'm going to have to use the speculum," said Dr. Rose, bringing the spider-looking device toward Amberle's eyes and forcing her eyes open with her thumb and forefinger.

"No," Amberle begged. "Please, don't." Amberle squeezed my hand.

"It's OK," I lied, closing my eyes.

"I know it's scary, but it won't hurt. I just have to get a good look."

Suddenly, Amberle loosened her death grip on my hand, and I opened my eyes to see the doctor studying her right eye. "There's a lot of damage," she said. "I'm inserting a Prokera® ring in your right eye." Amberle had worn a Prokera® ring—a corneal bandage resembling a large contact lens made of amniotic membrane—when she'd been in the hospital in Fort Worth. It protected the surface of her eye but severely restricted her vision.

"But I won't be able to see anything."

"Temporarily," the doctor said. "If I don't put it in now, you could lose your vision permanently."

After a few minutes, the doctor repeated the procedure in the other eye, with much less fanfare. She removed the speculum, and we waited for her assessment.

"I don't like it. Not at all. But I do have a thought. I just returned from a conference in Thailand where a doctor from Florida spoke about a new procedure—one that uses epithelial cells from the patient's mouth to heal the cornea. Like a transplant. It's experimental, but I think it's your only hope. Do you want me to call him?"

Amberle nodded. "Yes, please."

Dr. Rose looked up a number in her cell phone and called the doctor—who actually answered. As she explained Amberle's situation to the specialist, I prayed. I couldn't understand a word of the terminology, but after about five minutes, Dr. Rose hung up. "Dr. Tseng has agreed to take on Amberle as a patient, but time is of the essence. If we're going to save her vision, we have about two weeks. No more. When you get home, call his office, and they'll schedule the surgery ASAP." She handed me a small slip of paper with a phone number on it. "On the way out, make an appointment to see me again next week. Right before Thanksgiving."

"Yes. Thank you," I said, helping Amberle out of the exam chair.

"OK. I'll see you next week."

As soon as the doctor left the room, Amberle made a strange noise and began to cry.

"Honey, what is it?" I asked. "Are you all right? Do I need to call the doctor?"

Amberle crumpled into my arms. "Mom, I can't see anything," she sobbed. "Nothing. Not with this membrane. I've worked so hard . . ." Her words melted into tears, and I hugged her tightly.

"I'm sorry, but we have to trust the doctor, especially if we believe God led us here."

I handed her a tissue, and Amberle wiped her eyes. Taking my arm, we walked past dozens of patients staring at us as we made our way to the appointment desk and then, past even more curious looks as I pushed her in a wheelchair through the maze of hospital hallways.

We drove most of the way home in silence, but something was on Amberle's mind.

When we pulled into the driveway, she said, "I'm sorry I broke down, Mom. I don't know what happened. During the exam, it was so strange. When Dr. Rose put that thing in my eye, I didn't know what to do. I was so scared. Helpless. Like being in the hospital again. Then, I felt this presence like a heavy blanket surround me, and I knew being helpless was OK because the Holy Spirit was with me. But then afterward . . . I don't know what happened."

Amberle's words reminded me of a truth I'd learned in the hospital: being helpless is OK. In fact, admitting our helplessness is the first step in surrendering to God's holiness. However, as I considered the doctor's recommendation for surgery, I wondered whether we were putting too much faith in physicians and experimental treatments or if God was providing an answer through expert care and a unique surgical opportunity.

After talking and praying with Dee, I scheduled the surgery. The first availability was in twelve days, but we needed that much time to submit the reams of paperwork. The procedure would cost twenty thousand dollars per eye plus hospital and travel expenses. Since I had to work, Dee would accompany Amberle to Florida on November 28th. Dr. Tseng would evaluate her on the 29th, and if all went well, he would perform the surgery on the 30th. The nurse told us she didn't think insurance would cover the procedure since it was experimental.

It was expensive, but if it would save Amberle's vision, it was worth it.

†

Although we should have been celebrating that first weekend Amberle was home, we didn't. In the hospital, Amberle had made great strides toward independence, but now, without any vision, she was back at square one. At least, that's how it felt.

Admitting our helplessness sounded good spiritually, but in practice, it was wretched, particularly after Amberle had worked so hard.

At dinner, Dee tried to help Amberle by feeding her.

She exploded. "Dad, I'm twenty-one years old. I can feed myself."

When I brought her afternoon medications, she stopped me. "Mom, I have to learn to do this on my own whether I can see or not. Put the bottles and a glass of water on the table next to me and talk me through it."

Around 4:00 on Sunday afternoon, my friend Jackie called. "How are you?" she asked. It wasn't an idle question. She genuinely wanted to know.

"Well . . ." I tried to think of appropriate words.

"Wow, that was a stupid question. I can't even imagine how you feel."

I laughed. Jackie "got it." I struggled when people asked how we were because I knew what they wanted to hear. So, I usually lied. Perhaps the best response would have been "helpless."

"Gary and I want to bring over a meal for you on Thursday morning for Thanksgiving. Will you let us do that for you?"

I had plenty of food in the freezer, but I agreed.

"Great. We'll drop it off. Now, one more thing. I know you're swamped with the church musical right now. Do you need any help with Amberle? I can come over a couple of mornings next week."

I thought for a moment and realized being helpless was OK. "That would be great," I said.

I had to admit my need before I could be helped.

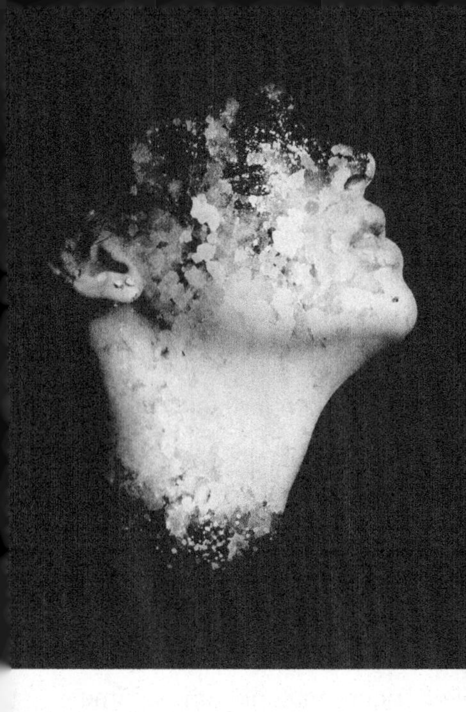

Chapter Sixteen

Thankful

The nurse handed Amberle a towel to cover herself. "I'm going to remove your shirt so I can see your back."

Before either of us could stop her, the nurse grabbed Amberle's shirt and pulled it over her head.

"Wait! Please!"

It took a moment for the nurse to realize her mistake. Amberle's back was newly bloodied where a piece of skin had been ripped away with her shirt.

"Her skin sticks to her clothing," I said.

The nurse, visibly upset, apologized.

"It's OK," Amberle said. "I'm used to it."

Dr. McGrew and a nurse named Skye came into the room. While Dr. McGrew examined Amberle, Skye took notes.

"I know there's more than meets the eye here, Amberle, and I want to help you in any way we can. As your primary care physician, I'll coordinate with the necessary specialists. Dr. Carrejo, whom you'll meet before you leave, will also be working on your case. Your mom just needs to make sure everything gets approved by Tricare. I'm going to give you about a dozen referrals in addition to your appointments in ophthalmology. Skye, get into the system and see what you can do about getting Amberle in before Thanksgiving or early that next week? Burn care is at the top of the list. And please ask Dr. Carrejo to come in."

After meeting Dr. Carrejo, we headed home. Amberle and I were grateful for the compassion of the medical staff and relieved at how easy the process seemed to be. "Now all I have to do is call Tricare."

"All I have to do...?" If only I'd known.

†

Over the next few days, Dee and I called Tricare multiple times. Time was short due to the upcoming holiday weekend, and each phone call came with a lengthy hold, an advisor who required Amberle's complete medical history, and a false assurance of approval.

"You don't understand. Tricare already has her information. We just need approval for her appointments."

Each representative apologized but insisted Amberle's information wasn't in the system. On Tuesday afternoon, I went into the bathroom and slammed the door.

"Enough, God!" I growled. "I've had it. Just give it to me. I'll take Amberle's pain. I can't watch her suffer anymore—while Tricare does nothing. Take away her pain and give it to me. Amen."

This was not a request; it was a demand, and I'd never prayed such a desperate prayer in my life. Weeks earlier, while Amberle was still in the hospital, Dee told me how he had asked God to give him Amberle's condition. I had not—possibly because I'd seen so much horror, and I was too well acquainted with the reality of it.

But now, I gave God an ultimatum.

Crumpled on the tile floor, I felt three words speak to my spirit: "Now you know."

"What do you mean?" I asked. The voice was so real and my frustration so great that I assumed Dee had heard me. Now he'd know for sure: his wife was losing her mind. But the room was quiet, and I was alone.

I knew *that* Voice. It was the same Voice I'd heard in the hospital.

"Now you know how I felt and why I came . . . as much as you can. I could not bear to watch my children's pain—on earth, enslaved to sin, and in hell, condemned forever—so I bore their pain, their sin, for all eternity. You would do anything to remove your child's suffering, including taking it on yourself. But you cannot do that. I can, child. I can and I did."

The tears I'd held back so bravely and for so long poured out. Tears of regret and relief. When I regained my composure, I went back to my desk and called Skye. She had scheduled multiple appointments for Amberle.

"You're a miracle worker, Skye, coordinating all these appointments. But we still don't have approval from Tricare."

"Amberle needs care right now, Glenda. Don't worry about the insurance. You'll eventually get approved. It's a convoluted system. Keep calling, and in the meantime, we'll see what we can do."

I didn't feel any better, but I knew Amberle needed the appointments—with or without approval. So, we went. Each appointment provided a small step toward recovery.

But still, no approvals.

I'd spoken to Tricare representatives every day for two weeks with no progress. Now, it was time to send in the big guns. The military. My husband.

On Wednesday morning, Dee announced, "I have an appointment with the Tricare coordinator on base. I know he can't approve the referrals, but maybe he can offer advice about navigating the system. I gave one-third of my life to the military, and there's got to be something they can do."

I kept Dr. McGrew's office updated, and they were nearly as frustrated as I was. When I called Skye, she said, "We called our state representative who's on the Committee for Veteran Affairs and told him it was shameful how your family was being treated. And Dr. McGrew personally placed a call to the White House. I don't know if it'll make any difference, but we're doing what we can."

Even if it didn't change the situation, knowing we had the support of our physician meant the world to me.

I took Amberle to her ophthalmology appointment, and Dee met with the Tricare representative on base. When he came home, Dee was frustrated. "They empathized with our situation, but there's nothing they can do. They're only in charge of referrals if we go to a doctor on base. Since there's no burn unit on base, it makes more sense for us go to UNMH. I'm calling Tricare now." My one-man army marched into his office, determined to win the war.

About an hour later, Dee came out of his office. "Has anyone at Tricare ever mentioned being assigned a case manager?"

"No. What's that?"

"Someone specifically assigned to your case who schedules all your treatments. The lady I just spoke to said she'd look into getting one for us."

I felt like I was married to General MacArthur.

†

On Thanksgiving morning, Amberle posted the following on *Caring Bridge*:

> *'Tis the season for thankfulness, and boy, have I learned about that! Isaiah 30:20 (NLT) says "Though the Lord gave you adversity for food and suffering for drink, he will still be with you to teach you." On the list of countless lessons the Lord has taught me through this season is the need and reason to give thanks in all circumstances, especially those that seem without reason. So here, I present my top ten reasons that I am thankful for TEN (toxic epidermal necrolysis):*

10. Seeing the core of myself in my unconscious while being refined by the fire.

9. Getting to eat ice cream at every meal (including breakfast).

8. The mercy of forgetfulness—in that God has spared me from remembering the most painful parts of my time in the hospital.

7. A million new ideas for inventions!

6. Firsthand experience to help me to become a more skilled, empathetic, knowledgeable nurse.

5. Meeting and getting to know incredible people whom I never would have known otherwise, especially my nurses in the Burn ICU.

4. Being the recipient of tangible love through the generous and thoughtful gifts, prayers, and words of my brothers and sisters in Christ around the world.

3. Precious, quality time with my mom, dad, Dr. Hawley, The Pitcocks, Lyndsey, Collin, Cheraya, Christine, Jessi, Sara, Kelsey, and many other precious friends in a forced oasis in the midst of a busy world.

2. Many opportunities to share the gospel and the love of Christ through my story.

1. The glorification of God through everything.

Bonus reason #1: Dr. K. :) ('Nuff said!)

Bonus reason #2: Mathilde's pumpkin bread

I could go on and on about how God has taught me to be gracious and grateful for TEN and for this season of my life. I've been told that I can get back to the plan that God has for me as soon as I get past this "bump in the road," but the truth is that this is an important part of the plan that God has for me. Perhaps it was for such a time as this that I was purposed. There is a season for everything, and now is the season to be thankful for TEN!

HAPPY THANKSGIVING!

Amberle

†

For me, Thanksgiving didn't feel like Thanksgiving. I could have blamed it on the fact that I didn't have to get up at 6 a.m. to start cooking, but in reality, I was disappointed. With me. I'd seen so many miracles, and God had been so faithful. Why did I still doubt?

The thought of having a daughter with a disability eviscerated my vision of our perfect nuclear family, and my pride struggled with the intersection of perfection and disability. Like a full-bodied woman trying to squeeze into a pair of skinny jeans, the idea wouldn't fit in my mind, no matter how much I squirmed. I wanted to be thankful on this holiday, but my ego fought against it. How could God's plan be perfect when my daughter's health was not?

Just before noon, Jackie and her husband, Gary, delivered a magnificent Thanksgiving meal.

"Thank you so much. It looks fabulous."

"Our pleasure," Gary said. "But we'd really like to help more. Lots of people would. I've seen dozens of posts from people asking how they can help with Amberle's medical expenses. I can set up a fund if you'll let me."

"I don't think that's necessary."

"It would bless us to bless you, and at least that way, we'd feel like we're doing something instead of feeling so helpless. Think about it, OK?"

I told him Dee and I would consider it over the weekend.

During our meal, we Skyped® Christina who insisted on carrying out our Thanksgiving tradition of each person sharing "things we're grateful for." At the top of everyone's list was Amberle being home. A close second was no more daily bomb shelter runs for Christina. Then came gratitude for family, friends, and examples of God's goodness in our daily lives.

As Dee prepared to close in prayer, Amberle interrupted: "I need to say one more thing. A few days ago, I was thinking about how God saved my life and how grateful I am. Suddenly, I felt God say, 'You've forgotten. I didn't just save you from death. I saved you from hell.' So, I'm thankful for what God's doing in our lives today, but I'm more grateful for what He's done."

We were quiet for a few moments as we reflected on a Truth we all knew but often left unsaid.

Yes, we were grateful for the recent change in our circumstances, but there was so much more to be thankful for. It was almost as if we were distracted by our physical vision, limited by our ability to see. Amberle, however, didn't have that problem. She could see beyond the circumstances, beyond the visible, as Paul instructed: "So we fix our eyes not on what is seen, but on what is unseen, since what is seen is temporary, but what is unseen is eternal" (2 Corinthians 4:18 NIV).

I didn't know what was ahead for us, but at that moment, I knew it was even more important to be grateful for what I could not see than for what I could.

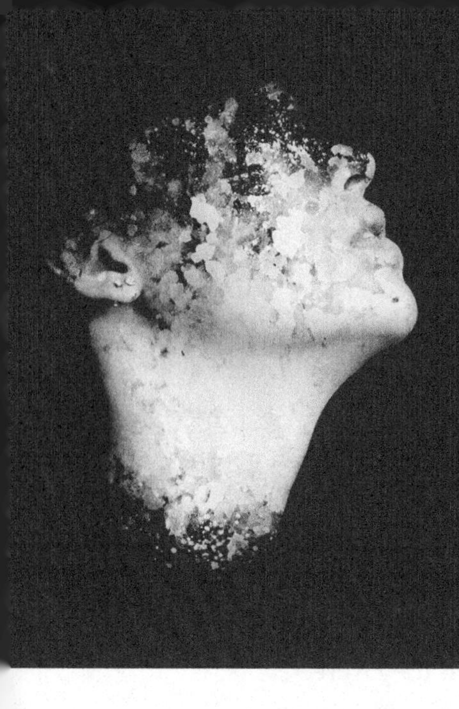

Chapter Seventeen

Reality

The caller ID was an unknown number, but I answered anyway.

"Is this Mrs. Durano?"

"Yes."

"My name is Karen and I'm one of the case managers at Tricare. I've been assigned to your daughter's case. How can I help you?"

I was beyond excited. After gushing my thanks and practically promising her my first grandchild, Karen asked me to explain Amberle's condition so she could have a better understanding of the situation. As I recounted Amberle's hospitalization, Karen seemed genuinely empathetic.

"Glenda, I'm going to do everything I can to help your daughter," she said. "Let's talk about her appointments." Karen assured me the seven or so appointments we'd attended without prior approval would be taken care of. All the referrals from Dr. McGrew and Dr. Carrejo were in Tricare's files; they simply hadn't been approved.

"It may take a while, but you can't delay treatment. Just go to the appointments. We'll catch up as soon as we can."

"Thank you."

"Now, about the surgery in Florida. I can't guarantee coverage for that. You said it's experimental, so coverage would be highly unlikely, plus, it's out of your coverage area. Florida is in our western region. You're in our south region."

"I know. But our ophthalmologist said it was our best chance of keeping what little vision she has left. We're going to do it whether it's covered or not."

"Well, I'll see what I can do. It sounds like your daughter has been through an unspeakable ordeal, and I want her to get whatever help she needs. I'll work on these referrals for the remainder of the day and get back to you on Monday. I'm not sure if anything will be approved by then, but go to those appointments as if they were."

When I finished the phone call, I took a deep breath. It felt like the first real breath I'd taken since Amberle arrived home. *Thank you, God. Thank you.*

Over the weekend, Amberle tried to wean herself off pain medications. She was miserable, and it was a bleak Black Friday.

"You don't have to stop your meds yet," I said.

"I know, but I've seen what addiction can do, and I'm not going to become dependent on these pills. I can do this on my own."

Amberle spoke out of her prideful stubbornness and her attitude was far from godly, but in a sense, it was good to see her strength. Amberle's tenacity was one of the reasons she was still alive. Once she made up her mind to do something, it was set.

I listened to Amberle toss and turn most of Friday night. About 3:00 a.m., I turned off the baby monitor so I could sleep.

Although I dreaded hearing the answer, Saturday morning I asked, "How did you sleep?"

"I didn't." Amberle described how she spent the entire night peeling away scabs, trying to expedite her healing, ignoring the searing pain. "I hate this, Mom. I really do. Sometimes, I wish I were dead. At least that way, the pain would be gone." Amberle sounded more disconnected than sad, as if she'd logically considered the options and made the best choice.

"Yes, your pain would be gone, but you'd be gone too." I sat next to my daughter and held her hand. For a moment, I felt more like a mother rather than a caretaker.

In the hospital, Amberle's pain had been much more severe, but the massive doses of medication had blocked both her pain and memory. Now, it was real. Constant. And worst of all, I could do nothing to stop it.

†

When one of Amberle's friends called Saturday afternoon to ask if she could visit Amberle, I warned her about Amberle's pain and her accompanying acrimonious mood. She wasn't deterred. Alyssa was one of the kindest souls I'd ever known, and Amberle loved her deeply.

"Oh, Amberle, you look beautiful," said Alyssa as she walked into our family room. "It's so good to see you!"

"You never were a good liar. I look like a homeless person."

Because of her discomfort and the propensity for her clothing to stick to her skin, Amberle was most comfortable in clothing nearly two sizes too large. But I knew what Alyssa meant. In spite of her unkept hair and mis-sized clothing, Amberle was beautiful—because of her spirit. They chatted in the front room while I worked at my desk. Soon, the conversation quieted, and I assumed they'd gone into Amberle's room. When I walked into the living room over an hour later, Alyssa was gently rubbing lotion on Amberle's back. Amberle was asleep.

"Can I get you anything?" I asked.

"Nope. I'm just happy to be here."

Not a word was needed. Her presence was enough.

Later that day, I was surprised by a phone call from Skye, Dr. McGrew's nurse. "I just wanted to check and see how Amberle was doing."

I updated her on Amberle's general condition and told her about Amberle's efforts to wean herself off her pain medications."

"That's one determined daughter you have."

When we finished the phone call, I sat in disbelief. *What kind of nurse calls a patient on a holiday weekend to check up on her?*

I knew the answer. One sent from God.

†

Amberle was already finished with her exercises when I woke up Monday morning. I commended her.

"This is the day things start to change, Mom. I'm going to do everything Dr. Hawley suggested so I can get back to school: walk, lift weights, write, listen to podcasts and Scripture, and turn on my brain. I can't control my life, but I can control me."

"You're right, and I'm so proud of you." I hugged my daughter and turned to leave. "Remember we have two appointments at the hospital today. We'll leave about 10:30."

"Mom." The urgency in her voice stopped me. "Do you know what one of the saddest things is about being blind?"

I didn't know—and I wasn't sure I wanted to.

"It's opening God's Word and not being able to see anything."

Amberle's words pierced my heart as I thought about how often I thought of Bible reading as a chore.

"But even though I can't see His promises, I know they're there. And I know God's fulfilling them in my life. Using blindness, God took me from a place where I didn't know what reality was to a place where I hated reality to a place today where I know reality is *not* what I see in the here and now."

Amberle's words were filled with truth and vulnerability.

"I'm grateful you have as much of His Word in your heart as you do."

"I am too. I couldn't bear to live without it. I hope I get to see again, soon."

After checking Amberle's appointments on the computer, it looked like it would be another day without referrals. "I trust you, God," I said aloud, trying to deny my disappointment.

Later that morning, Dee announced he was going to book the airline tickets to Florida. "I'll call the case manager before I do, just in case she's made progress." Thirty minutes later, when Dee walked out of his office, I could tell he was upset. "She seems almost as frustrated as I am. And she says her supervisor isn't in today." Dee shook his head. "I'm going to do some work, and I'll make the reservations tonight."

As I worked on last-minute details for our children's choir technical rehearsal, I noticed Amberle typing on her computer. "What are you writing?"

"Dr. Hawley calls it reflective journaling. She said it would help me come to terms with reality."

Reality. For Amberle, it could be condensed into one word: God.

> *I live in a world where dreams are more tangible than reality. Where darkness is more familiar than the light I see when I receive my hourly eyedrops. My recollection of my time in the ICU is foggy at best, and for that, I'm most grateful. I've seen pictures of myself that would make a sadist cringe, heard stories of sleepless nights, and seen scars that tell a story I would rather not hear. I remember dreaming of fire almost every night and trusting no one with their explanations of reality. But mostly, I remember an unexplainable peace resting on me at the most unexpected times. I remember feeling completely assured all would be fine, a positivity that, even now in my recovery, I can't replicate. And I remember a continual thankfulness for every moment, those of pain and those of relief.*

One might think the worst part of losing ninety-five percent of one's skin and mucous membranes is . . . well, losing ninety-five percent of my skin and mucous membranes. But that would be wrong. Spared through the grace of the Lord from the full extent of my lot of pain, the scariest part of my experience with TEN was my absolute disorientation. Even today, I remember my dreams a hundred times more clearly than my waking hours. In perhaps what was a protective mechanism, my psyche switched my dreams with my reality in my mind. I was convinced for weeks that my hospitalization was a creation of my subconscious—that my life consisted of parties at Michael Jordan's house, playing hide and seek with people I barely knew. Unfortunately, with little sleep and heavy medication, my dreams soon morphed into nightmares, always beginning with my ingestion of something that tasted like cat food. I faced strangers in hooded robes and dark basements. When the blending of these two worlds occurred, I began to think my nurses were abducting me or lying to me about my situation. It was like my brain couldn't handle reality, and I physically ached as I tried to figure it out. But my faithful friends and family continually reassured me of my status and safety in their loving care. Lyndsey especially tended to be the only one who could truly convince me that I wasn't dreaming.

Brutal as it was, I'm so thankful for the confusion that muddled my brain over the days of central lines and ventilators. I know God spared me untold suffering despite the difficulty I had mentally. I'm sure He used my subconscious to lighten the load I couldn't bear on my own. I will continue to question reality at times, knowing my psyche would love to create a situation in which I am so clearly the center of attention, but for now, I'll stop pinching myself and let faith be my guide.

Chapter Eighteen

Expectations

I glanced at my watch. It was already 10:00 a.m. "We leave for the hospital in half an hour. Do you need any help?"

"No. I'm OK," Amberle said.

I was annoyed when my cell phone rang. I wanted to check another task off my list before we left, but when I saw the caller ID was Tricare, I answered.

"Hello. I'm Dr. Cassul from Tricare. Is this Mrs. Durano?"

"Yes."

"I understand you're having some problems getting your referrals."

Some problems? That was an understatement. I was about to tell him in very non-Christian terms what I thought of Tricare, but God held my tongue.

"I'm just filling in today, and your paperwork came across my desk. I thought I'd try to help." As the stranger spoke, I began to believe him. I had no idea who he was or why he reached out. Dee and I hadn't spoken to anyone at Tricare except Karen who was doing her best as our case manager but seemed to be running into brick walls.

"I know time is of the essence, and the only way I can get an approval in time for the surgery is if you change your level of coverage."

"Approval? For the surgery?"

"Yes. But first you'd need to change your coverage from Tricare Prime to Tricare Standard. With the lower coverage, I don't have to perform the same level of due diligence, so I think I can get the surgery approved. Bear in mind, however, that would mean you'd have to pay twenty or twenty-five percent out of pocket for all future medical services, but Tricare would cover the rest."

I wanted to jump through the phone and hug the guy. "A portion of the surgery would be covered?"

"Yes, but you'd need to change your coverage."

I couldn't believe it. At this point, time was more important than money, but I didn't feel right about making the change without Dee's approval. Plus, Amberle and I needed to leave for the hospital in a few minutes. I explained the situation to Dr. Cassul and asked him to call Dee.

†

Amberle's appointment with Dr. Rose was disappointing.

"It looks like your stem cell deficiency is getting worse. I'll call Dr. Tseng and give him a heads up."

"Stem cell deficiency? What's that?"

I didn't understand her explanation, but the doctor's final words seemed more doubtful than hopeful: "Good luck."

Dee left a voicemail while Amberle was being examined. He'd spoken to Dr. Cassul and agreed to change our coverage. Amberle and I grabbed a quick bite before her next appointment, and as we finished eating, the phone rang. It was Dee. He didn't even let me say hello.

"Cassul just called back. He told me if Dr. Tseng is the only person who can do the surgery, we might be able to get it covered and stay on Tricare Prime. I told him Dr. Rose said Tseng was the only one, so I gave him her phone number. He's going to call her, and if she confirms Tseng is the only one, the surgery might be covered. Let's pray."

As Dee asked God for supernatural favor, I wished I had his faith. After the final "amen," Amberle and I headed to the burn unit.

"You've lost weight," said the nurse when Amberle weighed in.

"How much?"

"Five pounds, girlfriend. You've got to eat."

"I am, but I choke on my meds and throw up most of what I eat because of the scarring in my esophagus. We're waiting for insurance approval so I can . . . Oh, never mind." Amberle's voice trailed off into hopelessness.

We returned to the waiting room. Amberle slipped on her pink eye shades so the light wouldn't hurt her eyes. I wished I had eye shades so I could escape too. Instead, I decided to leaf through a recent copy of *People* magazine.

When my phone buzzed, I saw it was a text from Skye, Dr. McGrew's nurse. The bold, capitalized letters read, "SURGERY APPROVED!!!"

"Approved?" I said quietly. "Approved!"

"What?" Amberle said.

"Your surgery is approved! It's approved!" I hugged Amberle, and we both began to cry. Total liquid joy. "Thank you, Jesus. Thank you." Through my tears, I noticed other patients smiling, inwardly celebrating the joy of our hard-fought victory.

By the time Amberle was called back to the examining room, we'd regained most of our composure.

"Everything looks good except for your back. It's not healing the way we expected."

The way we expected? What did I expect? By now, most of my expectations had vanished, popped, and peeled away just like Amberle's flesh. But then, something unexpected had happened with the insurance approval. And it was wonderful. Was it worth the risk to hold on to expectations? To ride this dizzying rollercoaster of emotions—constantly swinging between hope and despair?

So many times, in recent days, heartbreak had wrenched us toward hopelessness. But then, as if we were in a supernatural tug-of-war, the Holy Spirit reminded us of all the things He'd done, like getting the insurance approvals. If they'd been easily accomplished, the Air Force would've received the credit. Instead, God put us in a place where He was the only way out, and although the memories stung, they gave us the strength to stand and choose hope.

"What can we do to help it heal?" I asked.

"Amberle should sit up as much as possible. Remove the pressure from the back."

"I do that now," Amberle said. "I sit in a chair in the den and work"

"Then I don't know why it's not healing. For now, let's just keep wearing that wound dressing."

"Let's?" Amberle was agitated by the idea that anyone would suggest her experience was cooperative. Only she knew the isolation and the agony of her situation. It was an unfortunate choice of words. "I hate this dressing," Amberle snapped. "It stinks. And I stink. I can't even take a shower, and I'm tired of sponge baths."

The doctor looked at her. "You can take a shower."

"No, I can't."

"Yes, you can. Remove the dressing. Take a shower or a bath and dry off completely before reapplying the dressing."

"But we don't have any dressing," Amberle protested.

"Now you do," said the doctor, grabbing a package of bandages and giving them to me.

"You're kidding!"

"No, I'm not."

Amberle sat in stunned silence, appalled by her own behavior. She lowered her voice. "I'm very sorry. Please forgive me."

The doctor smiled. "Of course." He glanced at his chart. "It says here you're scheduled for surgery. In four days?"

"God willing."

"You could be risking infection with all those open wounds on your back. I'd speak to the surgeon if I were you."

"Yes, sir. We will," I said. But as far as I was concerned, nothing was going to stop this surgery.

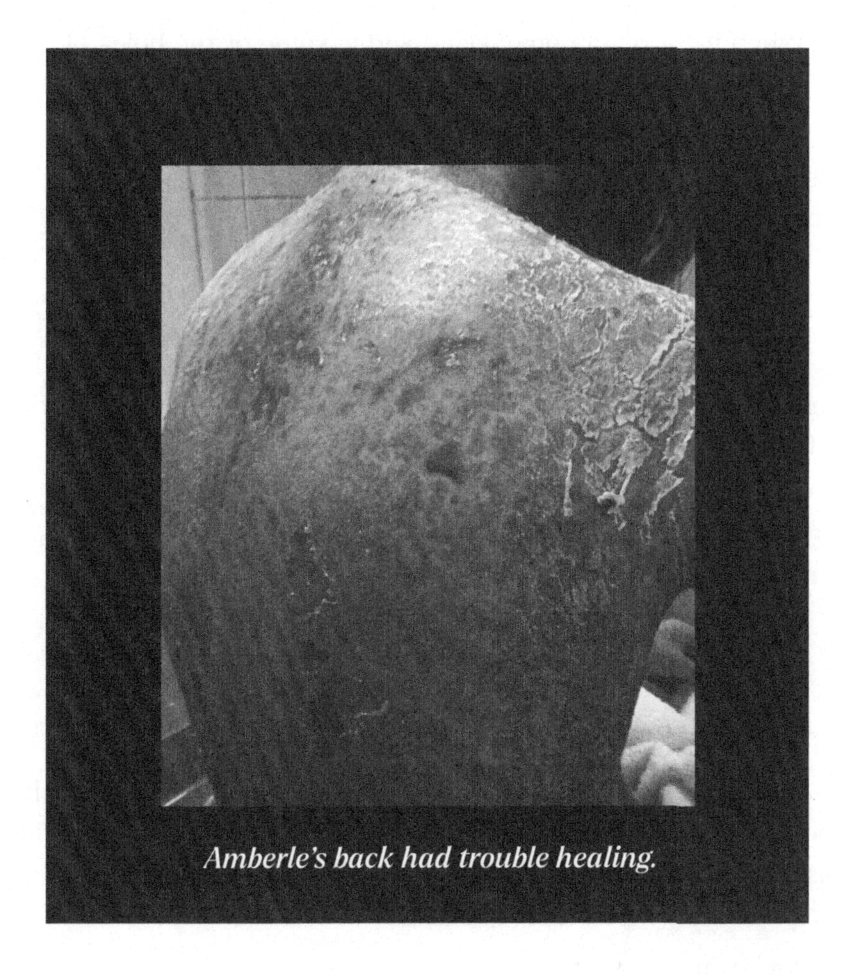

Amberle's back had trouble healing.

†

On the way home, I called Skye.

"It was the craziest thing. All of a sudden, every one of your approvals came through. All at once. And when I saw the surgery was approved, I wanted to make sure you knew. It's like it's..."

"A miracle," I said, finishing her sentence.

"Yes! I hope the surgery is successful."

"I do too. I'll keep you posted. And thank you."

When we arrived home, Dee filled in some of the holes of the eventful day.

"I'm not exactly sure what happened when Dr. Cassul spoke to Dr. Rose, but I don't think Dr. Rose was very gentle. He said she was very convincing—whatever that means."

"At least she's approved."

"Actually, she's only approved for the surgery right now—not the hospital. But Dr. Cassul assures me he'll take care of everything in the morning. And get this: Tricare will cover the entire surgery and reimburse us for travel and hotel."

"Oh, Father . . ." Words couldn't express my gratitude to God. "It's more than we could ask or imagine," I said, remembering the promise of Ephesians 3:20.

"Exactly."

I told Dee about the burn doctor's evaluation of Amberle's back.

"Maybe you should call Dr. Tseng before his office closes."

Jackie put me through to Dr. Tseng immediately. "I think it will be fine," he said. "In fact, I've been wanting to try a new procedure with this amniotic membrane. Perhaps Amberle would let me try it on her back to see if it expedites the healing.

"We're open to anything that might help."

"Very good. I'll speak to your husband and Amberle when they arrive, and they can decide then."

I hung up the phone and felt my heart beating faster. I felt more than expectation; I felt hope. And it was tangible, real, and completely worth the risk.

Chapter Nineteen

Progress

Wednesday was a flurry of activity. I helped Amberle and Dee prepare for their trip while several hundred TCU students fasted and prayed for Amberle's healing.

Although she'd been the recipient of thousands of prayers over the last few weeks, prayers that did "avail much" (James 5:16 NKJV), Amberle wasn't comfortable being the poster child for an anticipated medical miracle. She was grateful for the prayers but worried she might disappoint. On the day of her surgery, she wrote:

> *I can remember praying John 3:30 (NIV) for most of my life: "He must become greater; I must become less." I've always desired to simply be a vessel and a channel for the Lord's love, acting not in my own power but in His. And, as it seems from what people are telling me about my days of oblivion in the ICU, that finally happened. With my carnal self-sedation, God used my words and actions to glorify His name. Unfortunately, now I'm once again conscious, and my stubborn, depraved self is pulling for its own ugly way once again. It almost seems that I'm a more effective witness sedated than fully alert. Which leads to the fear that I won't be able to*

> *live up to others' expectations once I get back to school. With my mom's positive and uplifting stories and my friends' heartwarming testimonies, I feel like the general population of TCU expects me to come back with a halo and wings. Yet I've come no closer to sainthood since my illness, though for a time, I was a more willing follower of my Savior. But then, I remember that this isn't about me at all. This is all simply a testimony of the Lord's faithfulness and goodness. I was simply honored to be an actor in His grand scheme to be glorified and bring the kingdom to come on earth. All I'm doing is pointing to what the Lord has already accomplished and proclaiming the blessings He has poured upon me. None of this is about me . . . what a relief. Father, may I be minimized in all of this, and may You receive all glory and honor.*

No, this was not about Amberle. It was about God. But even with that knowledge, I struggled *not* to make it about what *I* wanted God to do, or what three hundred TCU students wanted God to do, or what a thousand other prayer warriors wanted God to do. I wanted God to do only what He knew was best. I prayed to align my desires with God's purpose, but in my soul, I just wanted the agony to end.

With this surgery, it seemed like God might provide a way out. I felt guilty for putting so much faith in a single surgery, in one man's abilities, but it seemed so ordained by God. Every detail, from learning about the surgery to having it covered by insurance, was beyond coincidence. I was willing to risk the disappointment and let God take care of whatever healing would be necessary after the surgery, whether it was Amberle's eyes or my broken heart.

After Amberle and Dee left, I tried to work on the details for one of our last children's choir rehearsals, but my heart and my mind were in Florida.

The pre-surgery evaluation went well. Amberle and Dee were impressed by Dr. Tseng's knowledge and compassion, and Amberle felt confident going into surgery the next morning.

"See you later," she said, as she was wheeled into surgery—with the emphasis on *see.* Her words were intentional and full of hope.

Dee provided me with frequent updates throughout the day. After the surgery, Dr. Tseng told Dee he was pleased with the result and pleasantly surprised at the state of Amberle's eyes, considering her overall health. Dr. Tseng had been able to operate on both eyes and repaired most of the damage with a less invasive procedure than originally planned. Eventually, Amberle would need more surgeries. For now, while her eyes healed, she wore Prokera® lenses, which essentially took away her vision. Dr. Tseng also applied a sheet of amniotic membrane to Amberle's back, hoping it would help her fragile wounds heal.

†

At the post-operative appointment on Saturday, after he examined Amberle's eyes, Dr. Tseng was more subdued. "I'm certain the right eye will be fine, but we'll have to see about the left one. I'd like to schedule a follow-up appointment in about six weeks. In the meantime, let's hope for a miracle."

We took Dr. Tseng's words literally, and we did more than hope for a miracle; we prayed. Although we couldn't guarantee God would grant our heart's desire, the possibility of Amberle being healed energized us. Over the next few weeks, Amberle saw enough improvement in her vision to know change was possible.

Since the two weeks leading up to the children's musical would be exceptionally busy for me, we asked one of Amberle's dearest friends, Emily, if she could stay with us through the first half of December. Emily had been best friends with both Christina and Amberle for over a decade, and even after Emily's family moved to Florida, the girls had kept in touch. As the oldest child of our former children's pastor; Emily had solid spiritual roots, as well as a sense of humor that kept everyone smiling. I knew she'd be the perfect person to help Amberle heal emotionally, and when I asked if she'd mind helping us out for a couple of weeks, Emily saw the request as an answer to prayer.

For several years, Emily had served in a Ugandan orphanage, but for reasons previously unknown, God had not allowed her to return this fall. Now, she knew why. Not only were we the answer to Emily's prayer but Emily was the answer to our prayer as well, and that became evident when Dee, Amberle, and Emily headed back to Albuquerque.

Amberle struggled with not being independent. She fought her vision loss and sometimes refused to be helped, insisting she could do it herself. We encouraged Amberle's autonomy but also fostered humility by letting her know that asking for assistance wasn't a sign of weakness. That was hard for her. Amberle's stubborn self-sufficiency sometimes resulted in close encounters with walls, doors, and strangers—who were no longer strangers after she bumped into them.

Before they boarded the plane to return to Albuquerque, Amberle and Emily went to the ladies' restroom. Emily offered to walk Amberle into the disabled stall, but Amberle said she could manage on her own. Amberle locked the stall door while Emily waited outside. After a few minutes, Amberle asked, "Emily, why is there plastic on the toilet seat?" Emily craned her neck under the stall door and, between gigantic chortles, told Amberle she was sitting on the trash can. They proceeded to play a sort of Blindman's Bluff with Emily trying to direct Amberle from outside the stall to the toilet inside the stall, with the emphasis on *trying*. Seeing the bathroom blooper with humor rather than embarrassment gave Amberle the ability to see herself as human. It was OK not to be perfect, and that acceptance was a critical step toward healing, for all of us.

> *With sight, we have the ability to determine our direction, choose our path, and avoid most obstacles. However,*

when you can't see, there's more to getting from point A to point B than just seeing where you want to go. You have to plan carefully and take it one step at a time, ultimately moving from moment to moment instead of from goal to goal. It's a different way of thinking about the future. And really, it's not a bad one—you plan your best, but you take life as it comes.

†

"The Great Christmas Giveaway," our children's choir program, was a huge success. It was Amberle's first opportunity to attend church since returning home, and although Calvary Chapel wasn't her home church, it was ours, and our church family had supported us every step of the way. Prior to the presentation, my supervisor, Roxie, introduced her and led the two-thousand-plus attendees in a prayer for Amberle's healing. It took everything in me to maintain my composure.

Completing my responsibilities for the church musical meant Emily could return to Florida. We would miss her ability to listen and love. It also meant I had to figure out what to do for Christmas. I hadn't decorated, purchased presents, sent cards, or planned any type of celebratory activities. But it wasn't just because I'd been busy with the musical. Our family wasn't even supposed to be in Albuquerque for Christmas. We were supposed to be in Israel.

Nearly a year before, I'd planned a Holiday-in-the-Holy-Land vacation, culminating with Christmas Eve in Bethlehem. It seemed like a great idea since Christina only had a couple of days off from school, and I figured if she couldn't visit us, we could visit her. But like so many other things, that visit vaporized. Christina and a few of her friends would use our hotel reservations in Bethlehem, and we would stay in Albuquerque.

It wasn't what we planned or wanted. But it did no good to be frustrated. Our exasperation didn't change the situation; it only confirmed our sinful, selfish nature. At the same time, we needed to acknowledge our disappointments and allow for discouragement. Finding that balance was difficult. But this was a journey, and God's grace would show us the way. All we could do was take one step at a time.

Chapter Twenty

The Gift of Uncertainty

Although TCU was on Christmas break, we communicated with the nursing faculty and administrators frequently. We needed to know what it would take to get Amberle back in school, whether she could still study nursing, and how long it would take until she could graduate. More than anything, Amberle longed to catch up with her cohort. We asked if Amberle might be able to walk during the spring graduation and finish her coursework later that summer. A handful of Amberle's professors agreed to give her half-credit for the fall semester and allow her to complete coursework over winter break in order to expedite her graduation, but in the end, we lost the battle: Amberle would have to repeat the entire semester.

TCU's response was hard to swallow, but the overarching question right now was whether Amberle would be able to finish her education at all. Would her eyesight be strong enough to finish her degree in nursing? Because Amberle still had Prokera® rings covering her corneas as part of her post-op recovery, we didn't know the status of her vision. We wouldn't know until her next appointment with Dr. Rose.

Amberle refused to be deterred by TCU's answer. Having to go through an additional semester of school was disheartening, but it wasn't the end of the world. Instead of focusing on the losses of the last few months, Amberle chose to embrace her lessons learned:

> *I can't say that my education as a soon-to-be nurse has peaked or is anywhere close to finished, but I can say that this semester, despite my medical withdrawal from "real" classes, has taught me so much about what it is to be a nurse . . . and more than that, about what it is to be a vessel for the Lord's love in any and every situation.*

†

Waiting for the unknown was exhausting. My friends' daily inquiries regarding Amberle's status—intended to encourage me—increased my anxiety. I stuffed it inside, sealed it with a smile, and distracted myself by putting up every Christmas decoration we owned.

With so much uncertainty surrounding everything Amberle had lost—her skin, her sight, and her school—and not knowing if she would ever regain any of them, I found it hard to focus on what we still had. However, with everything stripped away, Amberle did the opposite. She pressed into her new identity:

> *Skin is such an interesting thing because it truly does define you. As the primary component of your outer self, it can basically completely change your image, depending on its appearance. I'm fascinated to find the differences in my outer self I discover every day . . . my ears are no longer pierced, my stomach is a dark mottled brown, and my forearms have ranged from purple to pink in hue. The other reason I am so fascinated with skin is the parallels in Scripture I've found since losing my own skin. It seems that a whole new reality and truth have been revealed to me in the Scriptures as I daily find verses and stories that seem to directly relate*

to my physical condition. Many of these are regarding skin. I think about taking off the old self and putting on the new (Ephesians 4:22–24), like I feel that I've just done and how we are to "make every effort to be found . . . spotless" (2 Peter 3:14 NIV). In particular, I have found much comfort and belonging in the words of Paul in 2 Corinthians 4:16 (really, I feel like this whole book was written for me at this time): "Though our outer self is wasting away, our inner self is being renewed day by day" (ESV). It's also cool to hear the Scriptures about going through the fire, as I felt I did as a patient in the Burn ICU, and about eyes . . . "as we look not to the things that are seen but to the things that are unseen. For the things that are seen are transient, but the things that are unseen are eternal" (2 Corinthians 4:18 ESV). One of Jesus's most commonly cited miracles is the healing of the blind, leaving me with no doubt as to what He can do with my eyes!

Without the encouragement and admonishment of the Scriptures, I don't know how I would have walked through the refining fire of the last few months. God's Word is for us always, though I may not have realized just how specific it is to my life until now.

Amberle saw it first (as she often did without the distraction of physical eyesight), but eventually, I realized uncertainty was a gift from God. We just had to cooperate to receive the blessing and wait.

In my waiting, I was compelled to read God's Word. Like Amberle, I discovered truths that had always been there, but now, in the context of our situation, had new meaning.

In Isaiah 40:31, I was intrigued by the practicality of God's promise: "But those who wait for the Lord shall renew their strength; they shall mount up with wings like eagles; they shall run and not be weary; they shall walk and not faint" (NKJV). Certainly, I'd waited for appointments, events, people, and now, for healing and for answers—and those times were exhausting—but I'd never really waited for the *Lord*. Perhaps if I did, I would receive the strength, energy, and rejuvenation Scripture promised and I needed. I wasn't sure how to do it, but I noticed as I changed the focus of my waiting, life became more bearable.

Then there was Hebrews 5:8: "Even though Jesus was God's Son, he learned obedience from the things he suffered" (NLT). As those words traveled from my head to my heart, I realized Jesus learned to trust His heavenly Father during times of suffering—*because* of the suffering. The idea of Jesus having to learn anything didn't make sense to me, but I knew it was OK if I didn't understand the words with my head because God wanted me to apply them to my heart. Jesus learned obedience—the ability to totally trust and completely depend on God—*through* suffering. Perhaps I could too.

Suffering led to hurt and heartache, but sometimes, I inflicted the pain on myself by trying to rely on myself or man's solutions instead of Christ. Ultimately, suffering stripped my soul, removed my self-reliance, and forced me to see my relationship with Christ as my only Hope. That was the benefit of suffering.

I know the ideas I gained from Scripture weren't earth-shattering, but they were mine—revelations regarding patience, obedience, pain, and hope; found in the Word, confirmed by experience, and brought about by suffering.

That was the gift of uncertainty.

Chapter Twenty-One

Blindsided

I was almost scared to believe how much better life seemed. I'd grown so used to disappointments. Could we really be on the other side of this?

When Amberle came into the kitchen Sunday morning, December 16, her words confirmed it. "Today's the first day in a long time I feel like myself." No words were sweeter.

Amberle dared to believe things were getting better too:

> *I think I'm finally leaving the fantasy that this whole thing is a dream as I settle into the normal rhythm of life at home and regain my vision. In a week's time, even more will have changed as I believe I'll have my vision in my right eye and that my back will probably be fully healed! It's interesting how God works – for instance, the surgery that we HAD to have done in Florida because it was the only place in the country that we could get it turned out not to be needed because my eye condition was better than expected, BUT what other eye doctor would have had the nerve and knowledge to experiment with amniotic membrane to put on my back, which has truly expedited and assisted in the healing process?!*

The Lord's ways are much higher than mine, and I'm learning more and more that they always work for the good of His servants.

By the time December 19 arrived, we were bravely optimistic. We walked into the ophthalmologist's office, confident we would leave rejoicing in the good news God (and Dr. Rose) gave us. After all, when Amberle was discharged from Parkland, we'd been all but guaranteed Amberle would have a complete recovery and, within a year, Amberle would have no physical reminders of her bout with TEN.

As soon as Dr. Rose began her examination, it became evident things weren't going as planned. Blood vessels were encroaching on Amberle's cornea where they didn't belong. And although she claimed to be able to see some close-up colors and shapes, Amberle couldn't see the eye chart because the Prokera® rings hadn't dissolved completely.

"I can't make an accurate diagnosis until the Prokeras® melt. We need to wait a couple of weeks."

A couple of weeks? My chest tightened and that all-too-familiar "I'm-falling-into-a-black-hole" feeling came over me. In order to return to TCU, Amberle needed medical clearance as soon as possible.

"Is there any possibility you could remove the rings now, before they're completely dissolved? They've been in three weeks. Could you call Dr. Tseng and see what he says?" As soon as the words escaped my mouth, I wondered what boldness empowered me to say them. But to my surprise, Dr. Rose called Dr. Tseng right away. And even more startling, he answered.

Amberle and I prayed silently as they spoke.

Afterward, Dr. Rose said, "Dr. Tseng agrees we need to give your eyes a little more time. Let's try to get you in again on December 28."

Although I was disappointed, I reassured Amberle. "That'll still give us about two weeks to get you ready for school."

"School?" Dr. Rose asked.

"TCU starts on January 14, and Amberle needs medical clearance before she can re-enroll."

"No, you don't understand." Dr. Rose's voice had an edge to it. "Amberle will never go back to school. She'll never be able to read or drive or work on a computer. Amberle is blind. Permanently. Do you understand?"

I didn't.

"Not to mention her other health concerns. Mrs. Durano, instead of planning for school, you need to develop a good long-term care plan. Amberle's going to be an invalid for the rest of her life."

I stopped breathing. My confidence collapsed under the authority of her voice.

We were blindsided.

In an effort to help us understand the unthinkable, Dr. Rose described the chronic difficulties and daily challenges of visual impairment. The more she talked, the less we heard. Amberle and I wanted to cry, but we couldn't. Did we shut off our emotions to shift into survival mode? Disappear into denial, hoping the facts wouldn't find us? Of all the nonsensical experiences over the last two months, this one made the least sense. Dr. Rose hadn't completed her examination, so how could she be so dogmatic about Amberle's disability? Plus, Dr. Tseng had left the possibility open for another operation, an amniotic membrane graft, in case the first procedure failed.

Amberle and I sat in disbelief. We didn't weep or snivel or sob. A dam of hope held back our tears. But for me, possibly for the first time, it was not a hope in healing. It was hope in my unshakable relationship with Jesus Christ.

After she'd sufficiently shocked us into reality, Dr. Rose asked, "Do you have any questions?"

"No, ma'am," replied Amberle, with an unpretentious yet strangely congenial confidence. "Thank you for your help and your explanation.

I don't think we'll ever have any answers to our questions. And I guess that's OK. We just have to trust the One who does."

Dr. Rose was more confused by our response than we had been by hers. The look on her face divulged both bewilderment and pity. She paused, and not knowing what else to say, dismissed us with a "happy holidays" as she opened the door.

"Merry Christmas," Amberle and I replied.

I smiled as Dr. Rose left the room. It was a genuine smile—one that revealed *we* would be OK even if the situation wasn't. I asked God to forgive me for placing so many expectations in our circumstances. Again. And for demanding that God work according to my schedule.

I felt free in His forgiveness. Amberle did, too.

> *I don't know the last time the Spirit grabbed my attention like He did in that office. It's because of Dr. Rose, I thought. We have to be willing vessels in this situation as her eternal destiny is so much more important than my eyesight. I'm not saying I don't believe that God will heal me. I do . . . in HIS perfect timing, not mine. It almost frustrates me when people are so adamant that I will be healed. Honestly, I had put a lot of hope in my healing as well. But all that hope should be in the only One who can assure my hope, my Savior. I have sinned by placing hope in expectations and in what the Lord can do for me. I do believe He's not done working miracles in my life—physical and spiritual. I'm already learning much more about patience, His timing, and the kind and tender heart of my Savior. But my faith in Him and commitment to Him have absolutely nothing to do with whether He will heal me. There are no conditionals or contingents. He may, and I believe He will. BUT EVEN IF HE DOES NOT (Daniel 3:18), still I will not bow down to any other; still, I will worship Him. STILL, I will find my Joy in HIM, as He so clearly*

showed through my peaceful happiness after the appointment. The report may have been bad (about my eyes), but my God is still and ALWAYS, good. I am rejoicing in HOPE.

And yes, I cried.

Chapter Twenty-Two

A Light in the Darkness

I wanted to fast forward to December 28, but instead, God gave me practical training in patience. It was one thing to read about waiting for the Lord in Scripture; it was an entirely different thing to do it. The irony was that the tools I needed could only be nurtured in an environment that demanded them. Without a delay in Amberle's diagnosis, I wouldn't have needed patience, and if everything had happened according to my wishes, I wouldn't have found the promise of peace. But God, being God, knew this, so He used the day-to-day discomfort of the next ten days to teach me how to rely more on Him and less on myself.

Meanwhile, we did what we could to manage Amberle's overall health. The doctors in the burn unit were pleased with the healing of Amberle's back, primarily due to the amniotic membrane Dr. Tseng had placed there. The dermatologist confirmed Amberle's skin was regenerating well and, ultimately, the scars on her face would be minimal. Although Amberle hadn't brushed her teeth for two months when she was in the hospital, miraculously, she had no new cavities. After the ENT vacuumed dozens of pieces of dead skin out of her ears, Amberle's hearing improved significantly. And most beneficial in my mind, the gastroenterologist dilated Amberle's esophagus to help her stop gagging when she took her medication.

Even with this progress, staying positive was hard. Amberle was fiercely independent. My offers of assistance were often rebuffed with harsh words.

"I can do it by myself."

When I flinched from Amberle's frankness, I reminded myself that her stubbornness helped her survive. Tact had never been one of Amberle's strong points, but now, her behavior sometimes bordered on rudeness. It was as if, when her skin regenerated, an invisible layer of armor came with it. Fortunately, Amberle was abrasive only with those closest to her—her dad, Christina, and me. In a way, it was reassuring. She knew we loved her too much to be offended by her conduct. While I didn't enjoy being snapped at, I figured if I was in the same pain, I would've behaved even worse.

Christina called Amberle multiple times a week in spite of her heavy school schedule and the time difference between the US and Israel. Their conversations were always friendly, but nowhere near the depth of their "pre-TEN" relationship. One evening after overhearing a rather cold exchange of words, I asked Amberle a question. "Why are you so upset with your sister? She did nothing wrong."

Amberle exploded. "Nothing wrong? How can you say that? She never visited me once in the hospital. She could've come home, but she chose not to. Instead, she stayed in Israel, with her precious Stephen. She chose him over me." Liquid anger and hidden hurt flowed down her cheeks.

Over the last few months, Christina had grown close to a young man named Stephen Butler, another American pursuing his master's degree at Tel Aviv University. Christina shared their blossoming relationship through frequent photographs, and it was obvious they were falling in love. I was appalled at how the enemy could take the love of one daughter and forge it into a weapon to use against the other one through sibling jealousy. But he did.

As I thought about Amberle's words, I recognized a dagger of deception piercing Amberle's heart: the lie that Christina had rejected her.

Amberle had lost so much, and the idea of losing her dearest companion sent her into survival mode, lashing out at those she loved—a classic example of "hurting people hurt people." But Amberle didn't need a lecture on forgiveness; she needed grace.

Although it seemed impossible, the emotional fracture in our family proved more heart-wrenching than Amberle's illness at times, perhaps because this healing wasn't merely a matter of time; it was a matter of will. Amberle had to choose to forgive while the rest of us stayed diligent in our love, recognizing the influence of the enemy.

I tried to soothe Amberle as she wept. "That wasn't Christina's decision. Remember? Christina offered to come home but we told her there wasn't anything she could do here that she couldn't do there. It was our decision, not hers."

"She still should have come." Amberle sobbed.

"And drop out of school? Honey, it just didn't make sense."

Amberle pulled away. "You wait until you're in that bed and someone you love doesn't come to visit you. You'll see, Mom. It hurts. It hurts more than you know."

Amberle was right. I didn't know what it was like. The hospital. The hurt. The blindness.

But I wanted to.

Sometimes, when no one was watching, I walked around the house with my eyes closed. Still, my make-believe disability was nowhere near reality. When I opened my eyes, my vision returned. Not Amberle. The return of her vision was an unanswered prayer. Or perhaps more accurately, a prayer that didn't get answered the way we wanted.

To stay positive, we existed in a paradox. We blinded ourselves to circumstances in order to see the Truth. But when those very same circumstances provided hope, we eagerly engaged them. We could go through every emotion in a single day: joy, sorrow, anger, appreciation, fear, confusion, relief, surprise, and on and on. Stability became paramount, and we hung onto Christ as if our life depended on it. Because it did.

Walking out of church on the Sunday before Christmas, Amberle held my arm as we walked toward the car. "I could see some of the words on the screen, Mom. I've noticed it for a few weeks now. My eyesight always seems better on Sunday. That's no coincidence."

I made a split-second decision to feel encouraged. "That's great," I said. It made sense to me. If God could give Amberle a supernatural ability to enjoy corporate worship, why wouldn't He?

"Do you know what I see most of the time?" Amberle asked.

I assumed Amberle saw nothing but darkness, but her question led me to think I might be wrong. Ever since Amberle's vision had degraded, I hesitated to ask her about her sight unless we were at a medical appointment. Her vision loss was hard for me, and talking about it intensified the pain, but I was curious. "What do you see?"

"White. Pure light. It's not dark like everyone thinks it is. It's so much light that everything else just disappears."

"Really?" I thought of the Scriptures that spoke about God being Light. *My God turns my darkness into light* (Psalm 18:28 NIV). *God is light; in him there is no darkness at all* (1 John 1:5 NIV). *I am the light of the world* (John 8:12 NIV). Unabashed evidence of the reality of God's Word. In her blindness, Amberle saw light, not darkness, and the only explanation was the presence of God.

We had a quiet Christmas—a restful day. Our neighbor, Jean, had recently taught Amberle how to knit, and she was determined to finish her first project by the year's end. Amberle's newfound hobby required moment-to-moment concentration, which made her focus on the present instead of dreading the future.

On December 28, Amberle, Dee, and I arrived at UNM's Ophthalmology Department a little before 9:00 a.m. We sat in the blue-toned waiting room next to several people who appeared to be in their seventies. That wasn't unusual. Almost immediately, Amberle's name was called, and we were escorted to a large examining room.

"Good morning. How are you?" said Dr. Rose when she entered the room.

"I feel strong today." Amberle's words were a deliberate reference to the verse she'd been meditating on for the last ten days: "My flesh and my heart may fail, but God is the strength of my heart and my portion forever" (Psalm 73:26 NIV).

Amberle's examination revealed 20/100 vision in her right eye. It wasn't perfect, but it was something, and something—anything actually—was better than nothing.

The left eye was a different story. The Prokera® lens still hadn't dissolved which meant the cornea hadn't healed. My confidence faded. In spite of Dr. Rose's doomsday diagnosis at Amberle's last visit, we'd held stubbornly to the belief that, somehow, she might be able to return to TCU. However, if Dr. Rose couldn't evaluate her left eye, that would be impossible. We had to face reality.

Dr. Rose immediately called Dr. Tseng. I was so distracted by what this setback might mean that I didn't listen to their conversation. I didn't want to.

Dee and Amberle appeared to be praying, but I couldn't. Not now. My mind whirled in a thousand directions.

As soon as Dr. Rose got off the phone, she told us Dr. Tseng agreed with her that Amberle's condition was "highly unusual" and "quite unexpected." Then, she abruptly changed topics. "Let's talk about what you need to do."

I took a deep breath and glanced at Dee and Amberle. They were steady.

"Amberle will eventually need surgery again in both eyes. I can't give you a timeline because it depends on how quickly her corneas heal. Her right eye responded fairly well to the initial surgery, but both eyes need more work. Dr. Tseng will determine what's needed."

OK. Keep breathing.

"Amberle needs to adjust to a low-vision lifestyle. There are a lot of assistive devices on the market and trainers who can help you when you get back to school. It's possible that with corrective lenses your vision in your right eye could improve to 20/40. That's actually good enough to receive a driver's license."

"Wait. School?" I was certain I'd heard incorrectly.

"For Amberle's well-being, going back to school would be best. But she should take a fairly light load. I don't want her to strain that right eye."

The words were completely unexpected. *Is this the same doctor who told us Amberle would be an invalid ten days ago?* This was a miracle.

"So, I might be able to drive one day?" Amberle's voice trembled with excitement.

"I can't promise, but it's possible."

Dr. Rose gave us the address of a local business that carried assistive devices. "You can pick up a medical clearance form at the front desk tomorrow morning. And I'd like to see you one more time before you go to Texas."

"Oh. Yes. Thank you," I stammered.

I was overwhelmed by the change in circumstances, by the reality of a miracle. I struggled not to place my joy in the moment, but instead, in God.

On the drive home, Amberle and I were ecstatic as we discussed her return to TCU. Dee, however, was quiet. I wasn't sure what he was thinking, but I would know soon enough.

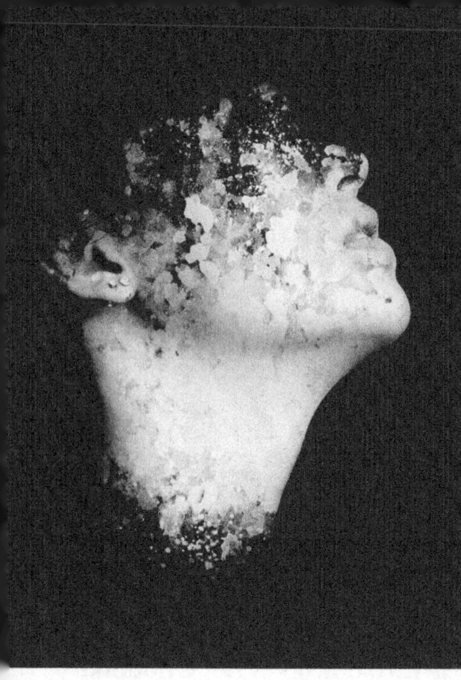

Chapter Twenty-Three

Faith or Foolishness

"We're setting her up for failure." Dee's words hit me like ice water. This was what we'd been praying for—what Amberle had worked so hard for. A sense of normalcy. A return to the life she so desperately wanted and, in my opinion, needed.

Now, Dee was willing to forfeit our dream—to throw away our miracle.

Thankfully, Dee had kept his mouth shut on the drive home while Amberle and I planned her move back to TCU. Our hope was no longer deferred, and we basked in the blessing.

If I was this offended by Dee's objection to her return to school, I couldn't imagine how Amberle would feel about his overprotective limitations.

"I want her to be totally ready and completely well when she returns. That way, she'll be successful."

I wanted to challenge Dee's response, but instead, asked a question—a question with an answer I'd been sure of at one time but no longer was. "What is success?"

The question hit the heart of our unspoken fears: destroyed dreams for our daughter and destroyed dreams for us. If we were honest, we'd have to admit, as parents, that a fair amount of our perceived success was tied to the achievements of our children. With that in mind, how did we view success in light of disability, and what did that mean for Amberle's future?

"Success is whatever you want it to be," quipped Dee, trying to end the conversation before it started.

"But what does success look like with a disability?"

Dee stared blankly ahead. "This isn't just about school, is it?"

"I don't want to define Amberle by her disability. But blindness is a part of who she is, and I don't know what to do with that."

I couldn't discount Amberle's disability. To downplay her emotional and physical pain was to ignore the power God gave her every day and to dismiss His mercy and grace. But Amberle wasn't defined by her disability either. Her sight was gone but her vision was not.

It was easy to believe the lie that disability and success were mutually exclusive. To the world, success is independence and self-sufficiency. But, as I knew so well, God's definitions and our definitions are often contradictory.

I understood Dee's concerns, and I recognized they were rooted in paternal love, even if they weren't necessarily true.

A part of me still believed in the lie of human perfection as well. My desire for Amberle to be autonomous was a sin. I needed to see her dependence on God not merely as something to be desired but as a vital part of her existence. And I needed to see it as a vital part of mine as well. Regardless of what ability had been removed from Amberle, God's promises were still true, including 2 Corinthians 12:9: "But he said to me, 'My grace is sufficient for you, for my power is made perfect in weakness'" (NIV).

Weakness. That's what disturbed me most about Amberle's blindness: knowing how difficult her life would be because of her disability. Unable to read a menu, find a friend in a crowded restaurant, or see directions to an airline gate. Was it wrong to want a life of ease for my daughter?

I forced myself to remember one of my most *a-ha* moments in recent months: *hard* is not the same as *bad*. The last three months had been difficult beyond anything I'd imagined—physically, emotionally, and spiritually. But in those same three months, I'd experienced God's grace "immeasurably more than all we ask or imagine" (Ephesians 3:20 NIV). If life hadn't been so hard, we never would've known so much good. Life had taught us a worthwhile lesson: you can't wait until life is easy to be happy. Live in rebellious joy.

No, Amberle didn't run from her blindness; she walked boldly toward it, knowing if God did not choose to deliver her from it, He would take her through it. With that attitude, success was guaranteed—with or without her disability.

Dee interrupted my thoughts. "You're right. This isn't about school or success. It's not even about whether Amberle's ready. It's about whether we're willing to trust God."

Were we willing? As we prayed about Amberle's potential return to school and discussed the pros and cons, we realized all acts of faith involve some degree of risk, at least from a human perspective. However, the risk that is required by faith—if it is a risk at all—is always worth the reward—a deeper intimacy with God. Besides, if God calls us to the risk, it's the safest place to be.

Although she was blind, Amberle was still "created in Christ Jesus to do good works, which God prepared in advance" for her to do (Ephesians 2:10 NIV), and Scripture promised she would be "thoroughly equipped for every good work" (2 Timothy 3:17 NIV). Amberle's success was not dependent on her ability. It was dependent on obedience, and as parents, we needed to give her the opportunity to obey.

†

Life was a flurry of activity: researching and purchasing assistive devices, planning class schedules, arranging additional surgeries, seeking academic accommodations, getting medical approvals, finding new physicians, and constantly surrendering our ideas to God's leadership in both the big and the small things.

By now, it wasn't the disability that derailed us. It was the details. We navigated the large obstacles fairly well; we expected them. It was the seemingly small issues that sent us tumbling head over heels, ultimately forcing us to our knees—things like discovering one required nursing class wouldn't be offered until the fall semester. Amberle had calculated if she took a full load during the spring and summer semesters, she could graduate in August, only a few months later than originally planned. Now, however, after speaking to her advisor, she realized her plan wouldn't work.

"One class," she sighed.

A few days later, when Amberle showed me her revised class schedule, she said her delayed graduation was probably a good thing. "It'll be better for me physically. And spiritually, it's another chance to learn one of the lessons God's been trying to teach me. I've been putting my hope in finishing school, but God wants me to put my hope in Him."

My sadness became surrender. "God always makes sure we learn His lessons. We never fail His classes; we just get to take them over again."

Amberle nodded. "I am disappointed, but I'm getting used to it."

The lump in my throat created a dam for my tears, and I recalled a saying: "Our disappointments are God's appointments." Those words had always seemed so wise and comforting, but now they sounded trite and cruel, like a band-aid administered to an amputee. *God, I don't want my daughter to "get used" to disappointments.*

Discouragement pounced on our hopes, trying to create enough doubt to make us reverse our decision. We had all the proof we needed to change our minds and keep Amberle at home, but we chose to look past our proof to God's promises. After everything we'd been through, we knew that proof was circumstantial at best, subject to change, and based on the knowledge at hand. God's promises, however, are eternal.

During those days, hope felt like a question mark. I wasn't sure what to do with the lingering *why* and *what-if* questions. I couldn't bury them because they were still alive, and like Zombies, they never died. They chased me down, ready to devour my soul, and although I thought I'd come to a place where I was satisfied with not knowing answers, the enemy still attacked me with uncertainty and insecurity, even when I slept.

Early one morning, I awoke from a nightmare. I'd dreamed Amberle had returned to TCU and failed miserably. This type of delusion had become fairly common for me over the last few months, so I'd trained myself to wake up before I was overwhelmed. I breathed deeply and tried to open my eyes, but that morning, my eyes stayed shut. I needed to know my dream wasn't real, so in my semi-comatose state, I asked the Lord, "What is reality?" I'm not sure what I expected Him to say, but His almost audible answer sent me reeling into consciousness: "I am."

Wide awake at 4:00 a.m., I realized what God had been showing me for months, but hadn't yet seen. *God's assurance is more important than my answers.*

I wanted answers because I thought understanding would give me a sense of control, but that lie had kept me dependent on myself rather than God. For weeks, I'd been chipping away at my paradigm's prison using the tool of human understanding, but, like using a spoon to tunnel through granite, it was a futile endeavor. Now, God's words shattered my shackles: "I am." My mind was too tired to insist on understanding, so I surrendered to His Spirit and embraced God's assurance.

Chapter Twenty-Four

The New Normal

Amberle was thrilled to return to the hugs of her friends and the purple world of TCU. Although her health was fragile, we felt secure with her new cadre of physicians. Dr. Hawley and Dr. Pitcock's wife, Jenny, lovingly shared the title of surrogate mom and agreed that one of them would accompany Amberle to every doctor's appointment. Amberle's vision had improved enough in one eye for her driver's license to be reinstated, but we all concurred the roads were safer when Amberle was a passenger.

Although Amberle's return to school was an answered prayer, it was not without stress. Dee worried about her success, and I fretted over the daily disappointments and future frustrations Amberle would experience while adjusting to life with a disability—both of which were relatively small concerns in the big scheme of things. However, once again, Amberle grasped what truly mattered and was determined to keep her priorities straight.

> *It's intimidating and overwhelming to think about what it will be like to return to "normal" life when nothing in the past two months has been normal. Will I miss the attention I was given as a unique and serious case? Will I forget the miracles the Lord has graciously*

> *performed and lose faith following my bent toward selfishness? But there I go again, worrying about myself. Nothing has truly changed because my God is the same today as He was on October 11. And as He has for all the days of my illness, He will continue to sustain me next semester and every moment of every day for the rest of my life. In Him, EYE rely. So, I pray I shall continue, day by day, decision by decision, thought by thought, to fade away until the glory of the Lord has consumed me.*

Although Amberle had been gone from her Horned Frog home for a mere three months, it seemed like a lifetime, and in many ways, it was. Her life was different now because she was different: disabled. I didn't like the label. I wanted to deny it and say everything was the same, but it wasn't. This was never more evident than when we sat down with the head of TCU's Disability Services to discuss the academic accommodations TCU offered to ensure success for visually impaired students. Doing this meant we had to look critically at Amberle's condition, which was the reverse of what we'd done for the last ninety days when we focused on what Amberle could do rather than what she couldn't.

TCU wanted to afford Amberle any assistance that would benefit her academically—an aide to take notes, emailed PowerPoint presentations, extended time on tests, and elaborate magnification devices. But to do that, they needed to know what was wrong.

I didn't like that word, *wrong*. It felt less than, as if something needed to be corrected. The more I thought about it, the more I believed Amberle's disability wasn't wrong at all; in fact, it was absolutely right. Amberle's disability forced her to depend on God and created a transparency in her life that allowed Him to shine through her broken places. Her disability demanded more of Him and less of her, and isn't that the ultimate goal? Although her blindness was hard and horrible, God had a purpose in it, and the sooner I trusted that purpose, the sooner I would be at peace.

Over the last few months, I'd revised my definition of *disability* to align it more with the degree of difficulty rather than a degree of defect, but I was still uncomfortable discussing Amberle's challenges. Satan tried to shroud me in silence and shame. The director of Disability Services recognized my reticence as soon as our meeting began and opened the conversation gently.

"Everyone has a disability," she said, "and almost everyone needs accommodations of some sort." She gestured to her eyeglasses to prove her point. "Normal is a just a setting on a hair dryer."

Disability was an omnipresent truth, not an individual curse. I'd never thought of

Amberle's blindness in those terms, but it was true. Everyone is disabled, and God alone knows the true condition of our bodies, souls, and spirits. Disability isn't an *either-or* situation; it's a *both-and*. Everyone has abilities and disabilities, and both are in the eye of the beholder. Some weaknesses beget obvious challenges. Others are more enigmatic and might not even be recognized by the person bearing the disability. In some cases, the disabled person doesn't give one thought to his situation because, for him, the condition is normal. Perfectly. Normal. Therefore, although technically, it's a disability; practically speaking, it isn't.

For me, the most freeing thought about a ubiquitous disability was the fact that the Creator doesn't love us in spite of our weaknesses; He loves us because of them. Genesis 1:27 (ESV) states, "So God created man in his own image, in the image of God he created him; male and female he created them." Every person is made in God's image, whether he's born with a developmental, physical, or intellectual disability or acquires a disability—including spiritual or emotional limitations—later in life. Pondering Genesis 1:27, I realized how little I knew about God's image because I so easily evaluated His image bearers—people—based on their abilities. I labeled characteristics as good and bad or strong or weak, based on my perspective, not God's.

My conviction to fully embrace disability became even stronger when Amberle pointed out that Christ Himself chose to be disabled when He became like us. I needed to accept my own and others' disability to have a more accurate view of and become more like Christ. Second Corinthians 4:16–18 (ESV) encouraged me: "So we do not lose heart. Though our outer self is wasting away, our inner self is being renewed day by day. For this light momentary affliction is preparing for us an eternal weight of glory beyond all comparison, as we look not to the things that are seen but to the things that are unseen. For the things that are seen are transient, but the things that are unseen are eternal."

†

Amberle found her accommodations useful and soon returned to academic excellence. Although school wasn't necessarily more difficult, studying was. Amberle fatigued easily, and when she didn't get enough sleep, her vision became blurred. Despite days when her eyes did not behave, Amberle still did well in her clinical rotations. Her experience as a patient had taught her more about nursing than any classroom ever could, and her new-found intuition gave her the ability to solve patients' problems creatively and compassionately.

Because of her ongoing vision problems, Amberle and I spent nearly every holiday in Florida, not on the beach as one would hope, but in the operating room at the Bascom Palmer Eye Institute. Dr. Scheffer Tseng, the physician who had performed Amberle's original sight-saving surgery, was determined to help Amberle regain as much vision as possible. Using cutting-edge techniques and tried-and-true procedures, he performed multiple eye surgeries on Amberle, some with limited success and some with no success at all. If healing could have come through human hands, I'm sure Dr. Tseng would have brought it, but Amberle's physical and emotional restoration was in God's hands alone.

Amberle saw physical progress weekly. Her fingernails and eyelashes returned, and her scars grew less noticeable. But underneath, a wound was still seething—a laceration that refused to heal, the result of what she felt was her sister's abandonment during her illness.

Now that Amberle was back at TCU, Christina called Amberle at least twice a week, but many times, her attempts at conversation were met with a frigid response. The tension culminated when Christina decided to visit some sights in the Middle East with friends during a school break instead of returning to the United States to see Amberle. Amberle was balancing a heavy load of classes and clinicals, so Christina assumed Amberle would be too busy to see her. Amberle interpreted Christina's decision as a flagrant choice of friends over family, particularly since Christina's new boyfriend was going on the trip.

It was a devastating ambush. Just when I thought the trauma of TEN was behind us, the enemy lobbed a grenade that threatened to obliterate my family.

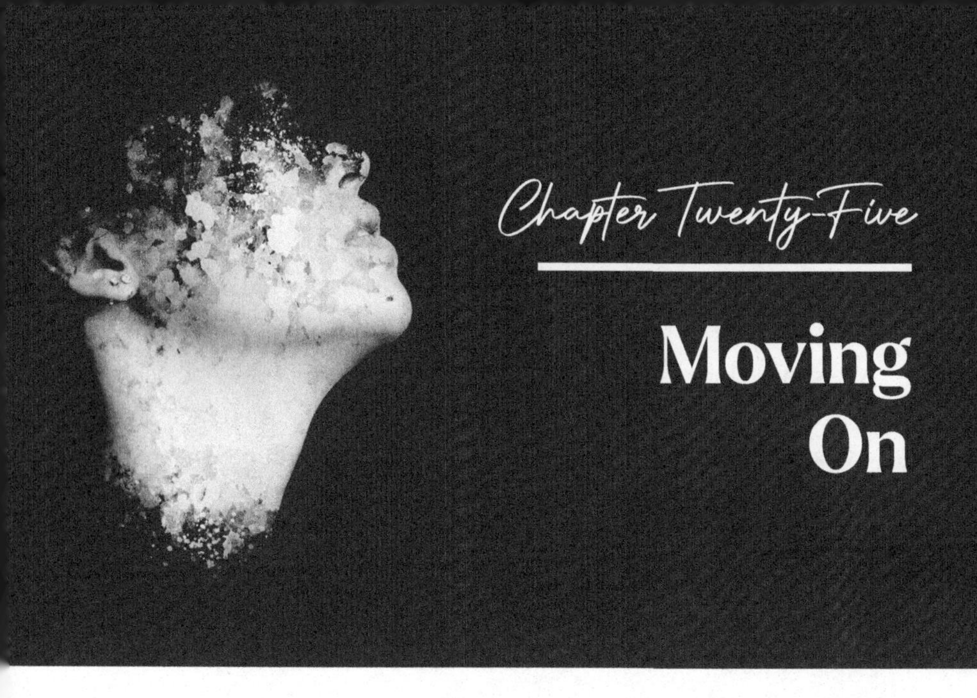

Chapter Twenty-Five

Moving On

April approached and with it came offers of good-paying jobs and postgraduate prizes for Amberle's brilliant and talented friends. She could not have been happier for them, yet each of their successes was a reminder of her suspension. Amberle forged relationships with her current classmates who were one semester behind her original cohort and gained new study allies, but she focused her energy on friends who would be leaving soon.

"Mom, guess what?" I didn't know whether to be alarmed or elated by the unusual, middle-of-the-week phone call from Amberle. Before I could speak, Amberle gushed. "I've been asked to speak at pinning. Every spring, the nursing graduates choose one of their classmates to give a final farewell, like a graduation speech, and they selected me. They had to get special permission because I'm not graduating with them, but I was approved."

"Oh, my goodness! What an honor!"

"It's a few days before graduation, and since you're coming to move me out of the house anyway, I thought you and Dad might want to come."

It was the first time I'd heard Amberle mention graduation without sadness in her voice.

"Absolutely. We wouldn't miss it!"

Dee and I arrived the night before the pinning. Fort Worth was awash in purple, celebrating its beloved Horned Frogs. Amberle had to study for a final, so we delayed seeing her until the next afternoon.

We shared long-awaited hugs when we saw Amberle. She seemed more like her old self than I'd sensed in a long time, but before we could get a word in, she was whisked away by friends who wanted last-minute photos with her. Dee and I perused the list of graduates' names in the program while we waited for the celebration to begin. Many of them had brought words of encouragement to Amberle in the hospital, and now it was her chance to inspire them. As Amberle walked to the podium, a woman sitting in front of us leaned toward her husband and whispered, "She was supposed to die."

I held back tears as Amberle spoke.

> *One thousand, three hundred, fifty-five days ago, you entered a classroom where you would become the unsuspecting members of an experiment. An observational study of what superhuman powers are fostered when first-year students are inoculated with a little bit of passion, incubated in a windowless building of Bass, exposed to other intelligent and insistent individuals, and inspired by the idea that, with newfound skills and practiced competence, they could make a difference in the world.*
>
> *The study began, and you were first placed in Lecture Hall 2, where if you could find it in the maze of Sid-Richardson, you were bestowed with the ability to write faster than you ever thought possible, and where your familiarity with fetal pigs was finely tuned. In microbiology, your ability to see the invisible was developed. In fundamentals, you began to learn the secret language that is dedicated to your mission, and not only that, learned to trust your fellow colleagues to give*

you a bed bath. You overcame the need for sleep as you studied furiously for pharmacology tests. And then you took on the signature uniform of purple scrubs, which you at first wore at every excuse, and later became less fond of. Released into the world of hospitals, you began spreading your contagion of care to your patients, learning all the while what to do and what not to do. Set apart from the general population of TCU by your familiarity with twelve-hour shifts and acquaintance with Harris Hospital's lunch menu, you became more and more close-knit as you experienced suffering and successes and changed bed linens with your eight other clinical classmates.

As you became more enthralled with the world of nursing, you noticed your non-nursing friends becoming more appalled at your ability to talk about any and every human secretion at the dinner table. For most, this was TMI . . . but speaking of acronyms, even those had changed – from LOL and BRB to COPD and BID. In fact, you began to speak entirely in the code language of nursing, which I still believe should count as language credit in the collegiate careers. As you learned about mental illness, you found yourself to be a prime case study of nearly every symptom discussed. And when you could no longer carry your twenty-pound adult textbook or the stress of the upcoming two tests, three masteries, and a presentation around anymore, it was the people sitting in the chairs around you today that gave you a hand. Now, after all those unforgettable experiences, you've been fully prepared to infect the world with the attitude and skill it takes to be a life-changing nurse.

When I last saw all of you in one room, I didn't yet understand the impact of a nurse—how having an excellent caretaker can truly color gloomy days and long hospital stays, and how feeling the support of your nurse can keep you going when the going is rough. Now I know. And that's why I'm so proud and excited for each of you young women and you five young men to be unleashed on a world in need of outstanding caregivers.

A wise TCU professor once said, "They'll never care how much you know until they know how much you care." So today, as you enter the world of nursing, you have the chance to spread your contagion of care to everyone you touch.

Whether you spend your nursing career holding babies or holding the hands of those who are breathing their last, each of you will be holding hearts. You may never understand the extent to which you shape lives, but even if your patients don't remember your names, they will remember your kindness and excellence.

As my peers, friends, and as those who have blessed my life in a more profound way than you can know, I am assured that you will change the world in immeasurable ways.

You will affect your patients' lives with your help, which will extend beyond physical needs to also reach the emotional and spiritual realms of their lives. You will inject your workplace with your heart for excellence and patient satisfaction. And you will infect the world with your hope, which will avail much as you persevere to not just improve the health of those around you, but of the world.

So here you are. You've made it through 124 class credits, twelve-hundred hours of clinicals, and countless bed baths. And what are the results of the four-year study?

> *Seventy-three bright-eyed graduate nurses with a fifty percent chance of talking about a body fluid at any given moment, who can pinpoint a stroke in their sleep and start an IV blindfolded. But the most significant result, more important than the mounds of information that would be found cataloged in your brains in any MRI, and more valuable than the passion running through your plasma, is the transformation that you've undergone . . . into real nurses whose dreams are highly contagious, who will make a difference in the world by inspiring hope in others – in your patients, in the community, and in each other. Hope for health, hope for excellence in practice and research, and hope for a meaningful life.*
>
> *So, as you go to infect the world with your big dreams and your contagious hope, I leave you with this final admonishment from 2 Peter 1 . . . "Now for this very reason also, applying all diligence in your faith supply moral excellence, and in your moral excellence, knowledge, and in your knowledge, self-control, and in your self-control, perseverance, and in your perseverance, godliness, and in your godliness, brotherly kindness, and in your brotherly kindness, love. For if these qualities are yours and are increasing, they do not make you useless nor unproductive in the true knowledge of our Lord Jesus Christ" (NASB).*

The crowd erupted in applause, and everyone stood in admiration. Amberle's nursing class would infect the world with their dreams just as Amberle had. Amberle's dearly loved professors on the platform offered Amberle congratulatory hugs, and she found her way back to her seat.

Again, the lady in front of me leaned toward her husband, "Do you have a tissue?"

†

Graduation week held all the pomp and circumstance one would expect, along with party after endless party. Amberle's situation was the epitome of "so close, but so far away." Rather than focusing on what could have been, however, Amberle submitted to reality and trusted God had a reason for her delayed graduation. Because so many of Amberle's friends wouldn't be in Fort Worth to celebrate her December graduation, they insisted Amberle join in the graduation celebration that was, in their minds, as much hers as it was theirs. The week took on a sense of joyous rebellion, with Amberle at the center of it all.

We whistled and shouted names and accolades as Amberle's friends crossed the stage with their decorated mortarboards. Most of the graduates had future plans or places of employment on their mortarboards for people to see. Nursing graduates' caps were slathered with words like "Baylor Hospital: Pediatrics" or "Dallas General: Obstetrics." Lindsey, Amberle's dearest friend, decorated the top of her mortarboard with "Fulbright Scholar–Thailand," but on the underside of her cap, she stenciled the letters, "A.G.D." for Amberle Grace Durano. The next day on Facebook, Lyndsey posted a photo of the initials with the caption, "Look who crossed the stage, anyway!"

Amberle had arranged to stay in Fort Worth the coming summer to work at TCU's Center for Evidence-Based Medicine, and through a connection at church, found a place to live with several girls while one of their housemates studied abroad for the remainder of the year. Some of Amberle's friends settled in Dallas for the summer, and their frequent get-togethers made the transition easier.

Before school started in the fall, I decided to take Amberle to visit Christina. Christina and her boyfriend, Stephen, had planned a wonderful tour for us from one end of Israel to the other, with every site imaginable. The only sight I wanted to see, however, was my daughters' hearts bound together again. The trip was filled with the wonders of the Holy Land and some true moments of joy, but Amberle's heart maintained a layer of protection.

Back in Fort Worth, Amberle threw herself into her final semester. Like many students, her final semester was a mix of anticipation and anxiety. Seasoned with the realities of her disability, hope seemed elusive.

"It's frustrating, Mom. I'll graduate summa cum laude with a higher GPA than most of my classmates in this cohort or the one before, but I'll probably have a harder time finding a job than anyone in my class."

"Amberle . . ."

"Mom, don't. I can't have any dreams anymore. They're too dangerous."

"Dangerous?"

"My dreams turn into idols. I focus on them instead of God. For nearly fifteen years, I worked toward being a missionary nurse rather than just drawing close to God. But now I know. My first dream, my only dream, Mom, is to know God. I have to surrender my dreams to Him in order to have hope. So, please, don't ask me what I'm going to do after graduation because I don't know right now. But when God tells me, I'll know. And you will too."

Instead of seeking an answer, Amberle chose a wiser path by seeking the Lord. She trusted God to direct her steps but knew she was responsible for walking. Amberle researched opportunities and prayed for direction. We respected her journey and didn't want her to feel she had to find an answer for our sake. As hard as it was, Dee and I decided to keep our mouths shut and our Spirits open.

In mid-September, Amberle called us. "The more I pray about it, the more convinced I am that I'm still supposed to do something in the medical field."

Although her vision was better now, Dee and I couldn't understand how someone with only one functioning eye could work in medicine—even if she was our incredible, amazing daughter. We didn't want to discourage her, but we wanted to be realistic. "How can you do that, honey?"

"I'm thinking about studying public health. A lot of medical missionaries study it because it gives them practical tools to help marginalized populations. It focuses on teaching people how to make wise choices for their health if they're facing a situation like poverty or pregnancy or living with a disease like typhoid or TB. If I get a master's degree in public health, I can educate aspiring missionaries. It would be the next best thing to being in the field because I can share my passion with others."

Amberle didn't need to sell us on the idea. We knew she had researched and prayerfully considered her options. "Johns Hopkins is the number one school for public health. It offers dual degrees that combine a master of science in nursing with a master in public health. I want to apply, if it's OK with you."

Because Amberle had received a full-tuition scholarship from TCU, she still had nearly enough money to pay for a graduate degree in her college fund. We agreed to pray about the decision with her.

A few weeks later, Amberle submitted her application to Johns Hopkins University.

†

On October 11, 2013, Amberle marked her one-year anniversary by posting a public letter on Facebook.

> *My treasured family,*
>
> *Three-hundred sixty-five days, three surgeries, seventeen fuzzy blankets, two-and-a-half journals, four-hundred-plus Starbursts, five bottles of sunscreen, more than a few dozen compassionate nurses and doctors, and one fateful pill ago, I sat here, a girl with clear corneas but a cloudy heart. With a well-perpetuated illusion of control and contentment found in my résumé. With surface-level joy and misplaced hope.*

I could say a single pill changed my life. I could say that if I hadn't taken that ibuprofen or if I hadn't been misdiagnosed, I might be the same person I was a year ago. But I am so thankful for that pill.

Because I am not the same. Physically, my new epidermis and stem cell transplant are not the defining characteristics of newness. The truth is, you changed my life. Today, I'm struggling to find words to portray the gratitude I feel because a loving God knew exactly what people He would use to remind me of His constant faithfulness and steadfast love.

I remember one of my saddest moments when I was recuperating was when I opened my Bible only to see what looked like empty pages. Even though those pages looked starkly white, they were filled with promises I had yet to believe, promises that, despite my inability to see them, God was already fulfilling. He's brought me from a place where I didn't know what reality was to a place where I hated reality to a place where I realize that reality is not what I see here and now anyway. And, today, on my year anniversary, I want to say thank you.

In God's abundant love, He put a community around me that would share in my burden when I began to lose hope and would point me toward the cross when I got caught up in my life. You played an irreplaceable role in saving my life and encouraging me to see Hope.

With love irrevocable,

Amberle

†

Amberle's excitement about her acceptance into Johns Hopkins' January 2014 master of science in nursing/master of public health dual degree program was hijacked when her medical team recommended several urgent eye surgeries. The surgeries entailed staying in Dallas for post-operative care which meant Amberle couldn't be in Baltimore in time to begin her studies at Johns Hopkins. Of course, Amberle's vision took priority, so she prepared herself for another disappointment and called JHU graduate admissions.

"Your situation's unique," the admissions director said, "but we think you're an excellent candidate for the program. You could defer until the summer of 2015. Would that give you enough time for your recovery?"

Amberle couldn't believe her ears. "Yes. Yes, it would." It was an obstacle turned into an opportunity and, although we didn't know it, an improbable, providential path.

†

Several weeks before her December 2013 graduation, Amberle called. "I've been offered a job working in the ICU at Baylor Hospital in Dallas. What do you think?" It was the perfect situation. Amberle could have her medical procedures without having to travel, and one of her closest friends, Kathryn, had invited her to live with her in Dallas. The administration at Baylor Hospital knew about Amberle's visual impairment, but they felt her abilities outweighed her disability. So, she accepted the offer.

Amberle looked like a WWE wrestling champion with all her medallions around her neck at graduation. Diane and Mom flew in from Oklahoma City, and we even managed a surprise appearance from Christina, who wouldn't have missed Amberle's graduation for the world. We invited a dozen of her friends who were still in the area to join us for dinner and a celebration. "Pomp and Circumstance" always stirred my heart, but I had to blink back tears as Amberle marched down the aisle to do something that seemed like an impossibility not so long ago. When she crossed the stage, a yell went up for all heaven to hear.

Chancellor Boschini paused for a traditional graduation picture with Amberle, smiled like a proud father, and offered Amberle the secret Chancellor's Scholar handshake.

Amberle's adoring friends, family, and fans met her outside the auditorium. They lavished her with congratulatory words; long, heart-felt hugs; and bouquets of flowers and cards. When Amberle wrapped her arms around my neck, she began to sob, and I did too. It seemed the only reasonable response to a miracle.

†

Christina had asked if Stephen could join our family for the Christmas holidays. After graduating from Tel Aviv University, Christina and Stephen had volunteered with Syrian refugees in Jordan, and now they were interning at the State Department in Washington, DC. Christina told us Stephen wanted to "talk to Dee about something," so we figured the trip was more than just a casual holiday visit. We were right. Before Stephen spoke to Dee, however, he took Amberle to coffee. Stephen's graduate degree was in peace and conflict resolution, and he needed every bit of his ability to broach the subject of his pending marriage to Christina with Amberle.

"I know you don't like me, Amberle, and I'm sorry about that. I can't imagine what you've been through, but I promise I never tried to steal Christina from you. I'm going to ask your dad for Christina's hand, and I think he'll say yes. But first, I want your blessing. You love Christina, and I love Christina. So, for her benefit, we need to work out our problems. I'm going to marry your sister, Amberle, and I'd like your blessing."

Albeit grudgingly, Amberle gave her approval. Dee also gave his permission, and the wedding was set for late March of the following year.

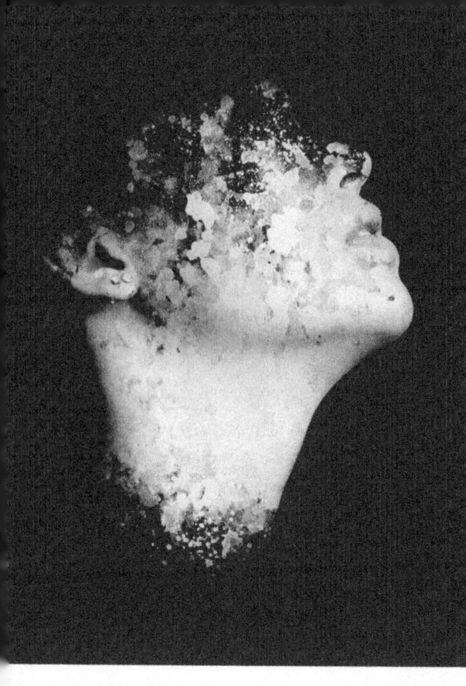

Chapter Twenty-Six

On the Other Side

The past was passed. Lesson learned. Chapter finished.

We thought.

In January, Amberle moved into an apartment with a dear friend from TCU, Kathryn. She settled into her job as an ICU nurse, working three twelve-hour shifts per week. It was a better-than-ideal schedule since Amberle still had two or three doctor's appointments every week. Amberle's ophthalmologist, Dr. Bowman, monitored her roller-coaster vision carefully and conferred frequently with Dr. Tseng, but the instability was mystifying. Whenever her vision diminished, a new prescription for her glasses seemed to solve the problem. Until it didn't.

"Let's try a scleral lens," her optometrist suggested.

Immediately, Amberle's acuity improved to 20/40 in her working eye. "How did I manage to work in the ICU without it?"

We should have taken Amberle's query more seriously, but it was a case of "if you can't stand the answer, don't ask the question." So, we didn't ask. We were just happy Amberle had her life back.

Part of that life included dating Hunter Brown. Hunter had grown up with one of Amberle's friends, Shelby, and had graduated in May from the University of Texas at Arlington. An amateur chef, Hunter loved cooking. Throughout college, he occasionally prepared "forty-year-old dinners" (so named for the upscale, multi-course dinners he served) for Shelby and her friends. Hunter had wanted to ask Amberle out since he'd first met her during their freshman year, but it was common knowledge that one of Amberle's requirements for a viable suitor was someone who was called to the mission field. Hunter was not. He was called to the golf course, and his dream was to work his way up through the ranks of the PGA.

Amberle told Dee that Hunter would be calling him to ask his permission to date her. That was part of our courtship model. Dating was not recreational; it was exploratory—for marriage. Throughout high school and college, whenever a young man became interested in either of our girls, we asked Christina or Amberle, "Are you ready to get married?" Until then, the answer had always been a clear *no* from Amberle, but when Hunter came calling, she told us she was ready to explore a permanent relationship. We were both flummoxed by her choice: a golfer?

When Hunter called Dee to ask if he could date Amberle, Dee's first question to him was, "What are your intentions?" Hunter answered respectfully, expressing his desire to get to know Amberle better. Pleased with Hunter's reply, Dee continued, "Why do you want to marry her?"

The question would have sent most potential suitors packing, but Hunter responded with ease and grace. Later, Amberle would tell the story of their first disastrous date, how Hunter addressed her as "dude," and didn't open the car door for her or help her with her coat. At the end of the night, when Hunter asked if he could see her again, she responded, "Are you kidding? No way."

Although Amberle didn't have a lot of knowledge about dating, she knew this was not the beginning of a fairytale relationship. Hunter had little dating experience as well, so he was completely ignorant. Clueless, he begged for mercy. "Please, tell me what I did wrong. I can change."

Amberle's up-front communication let Hunter know exactly what she expected. Basically, "nothing like tonight." Hunter was crushed to tears, apologized multiple times, and asked if they could pray together. After a two-hour-long heart-to-heart, Hunter begged for another chance. Touched by what seemed like sincere repentance, Amberle agreed to one more date.

The relationship blossomed, nourished by long walks through the Dallas Botanical Gardens and fireside chats about the writings of C. S. Lewis and A. W. Tozer. Amberle found a safe place with Hunter and even invited him to accompany her to Christina's and Stephen's wedding in Florida at the end of March. Because Amberle was still working through her resentment of Stephen, Amberle's role as Christina's maid of honor was challenging. Fortunately, Hunter's reassuring presence gave Amberle the emotional stability she needed for the wedding.

†

Shortly after Christina's wedding, the answer to the question none of us had been brave enough to ask became clear. Dr. Bank, Amberle's optometrist, delivered the news.

"The scleral lens is causing corneal swelling," he said. "I don't recommend wearing it more than three hours a day, and even then, it may result in total vision loss."

The idea of Amberle's vision being viable only three hours a day brought us face-to-face with reality. What would that mean for Amberle's graduate school, future career, or ability to function independently as an adult? The questions ripped the barely formed scabs off what we thought were our healed hearts, revealing our bloody wounds again.

This time, however, we recognized our pain for what it was. An opportunity. A heart-wrenching, tear-filled, yes-Lord-I-trust-you opportunity. Whether or not we could not fully surrender to that opportunity, however, was uncertain. We tried not to panic as Amberle continued visiting befuddled specialists, and each appointment produced more questions and no answers.

Amberle struggled with her sight for the next few months. At work, she excused herself multiple times a day to clean and reposition her lens, many times with no improvement. One evening on the phone, she confessed her concern. "I'm not sure I can trust myself anymore. It's hard to read the charts, and I don't want to endanger my patients. Maybe it's time for me to do . . . something else."

Was it defeat or surrender in her voice? Amberle had worked so hard and had overcome so much. And now, this. Again. A familiar fear rose within me. I stuffed it down, refusing to be manipulated by threats of failure. "We'll support whatever decision you make."

But Amberle never made the decision. Several days later, she called me as she was driving home from work.

"Hi Mom." Her voice sounded different, but I couldn't place the emotion.

"Hey, sweetie. What's up?"

"Ummm . . . I wanted to let you know I was driving home and had to pull to the side of the road."

"Oh, dear. Is something wrong with your car? Maybe you can call Hunter and he can come and pick you up."

"I did call him, Mom," she reassured me. "He's on his way."

"Good, honey."

Amberle took a breath, and I assumed she was going to tell me she'd been in an accident, but she didn't. "Nothing's wrong with the car."

I was relieved but still confused why she was calling.

"I pulled to the side of the road because . . . I can't see anything."

I heard the words, but they made no sense. "What?"

"I can't see anything. It's just . . . dark. Something's wrong."

It was our worst fears come true.

I stayed on the phone with Amberle until Hunter arrived which, thankfully, wasn't long. We prayed together, and I asked a few questions, but Amberle had no answers. She'd done nothing different that day and had no explanation for her sudden vision loss. Hopefully, Dr. Bowman would.

†

Amberle and Hunter were in Dr. Bowman's office at 9 a.m. the next morning. Fortunately, Amberle had regained a little vision overnight. Because of Amberle's fragile eyesight, Dr. Bowman was always quick to fit her in, and over the last few months, they'd developed a strong doctor-patient relationship.

"The corneas are swollen, but that doesn't account for the blindness." Dr. Bowman was perplexed. After several other evaluations, he performed an intraocular pressure test—an exam that measures the fluid pressure in the eye. He sat back on his stool and made an educated guess. "I think I know what might have happened, Amberle. When your eye tissue sloughed off, it clogged your drainage ducts and put pressure on the ocular nerve, causing it to deteriorate. Without a healthy ocular nerve, the brain can't receive visual signals. We've been focusing on keeping your corneas healthy, but it looks like you may have developed glaucoma now, which is much more serious." He shook his head, as if refusing to believe his own diagnosis. "We like to see pressure in the low twenties for people your age, and your intraocular pressure is . . ." Dr. Bowman glanced at his notes, hoping the numbers had magically changed, ". . . in the high thirties. I'm going to refer you to a glaucoma specialist, Dr. Michelle Butler. She's excellent. We'll make an appointment for you later this morning and see what she has to say."

The pastel blue walls and cream-colored chairs in Dr. Butler's waiting room did nothing to ease Amberle's angst. Neither did the fact that not one patient appeared to be under age sixty. Again, Amberle was an anomaly. Dr. Butler recommended immediate surgery, and while the procedure itself wouldn't be a problem, the recovery process was—four weeks of lifting no more than twenty pounds. As an ICU nurse, Amberle lifted patients weighing one-hundred-plus pounds daily. Because readings for intraocular pressure could be unreliable, Amberle scheduled another test the next morning. Miraculously, her pressure had dropped fifteen points and her vision had improved, so Dr. Butler delayed the surgery.

Amberle continued working, and intraocular pressure tests became part of her regimen. In August, however, the pressure in Amberle's eyes skyrocketed, and Dr. Butler surgically implanted drainage tubes in Amberle's eyes to relieve the pressure on her ocular nerve. Amberle went on short-term disability.

God had done so much for us. This made no sense. After all we'd been through, why would He allow this? Why would He permit such miraculous healing, such magnificent opportunities to glorify Him, only to reverse the situation and send Amberle plunging into darkness? I had no defense for God's actions. No answers. Every uncertainty I'd had since October 11, 2012—the day Amberle entered the hospital—fused into one enormous question. It was the question I needed the answer to—the question I'd asked hundreds of times before and the question I'd forced myself *not* to ask just as many if not more times. It was the question the disciples asked Jesus on the Sea of Galilee (Mark 4:35-41): "Lord, don't you care?"

Although my head knew the answer—of course, God cares—circumstances tried to convince my heart otherwise. Even at this point, it would take months for me to fathom the Truth, to appreciate how and why God would permit a lifetime of suffering for His children.

Blindness would be hard—it would bring pain and difficulty—but Amberle's blindness did not mean God didn't care. God wanted me to move past everything I thought of as proof of His love—all the blessings of health and happiness—in order to discover the promise of love: His relationship with me.

As before, I pleaded with God to take away the tempest, but He did not. He loved me too much to rescue me. God knew the only way I could discover stability and rid myself of this emotional whiplash was to go through the storm.

At one point, I was certain God had allowed the glaucoma so that when He miraculously healed Amberle, it would be hailed as a miracle rather than a surgical solution. But that never happened. I wish I could say I'd learned all the lessons God had taught me the first time around, but obviously, I had not. I didn't yet realize God's children don't live by explanations. We live by promises.

So, I found myself asking the same questions. Having that all-too-familiar sense of what if and why? Perhaps they were slightly wiser versions of the questions, but they were questions, nonetheless. I chided myself for asking them, believing my questions indicated a weak faith. What I didn't realize is that questions indicate you haven't given up hope. And hope is critical to healing.

It wasn't until years later that I realized the reason for our repeat lesson: LOVE.

If we could have learned the lesson any other way, with less pain and diminished suffering, I believe God would have done it. But our Creator knows us, and He knows exactly what it takes to mold us into a closer likeness of Himself.

Chapter Twenty-Seven

No Is a Direction

Although some physical healing came after Amberle's first glaucoma surgery, her emotional state deteriorated. She felt like "a worthless blob."

Nothing we said alleviated her angst. Unfortunately, the follow-up appointments for her surgery indicated that, while the insertion of the tubes would slow down the disappearance of her vision, Amberle had already lost almost eighty-five percent of it. The pain in Amberle's eyes was much worse now than it had been before the glaucoma surgery, so we agreed to another surgical procedure that promised and ultimately delivered some relief.

Dr. Butler tried to be encouraging. "Time is the best healer."

I had a love-hate relationship with the word *time*. In the hospital, Satan had convinced me time was frozen, motionless. That nothing would ever change for Amberle, except perhaps for the situation to worsen. God had proven the opposite, and we needed to remember that. Life always changed. The only thing that never changed was God Himself.

Although she was eager to go back to work and somehow prove her worthiness, Amberle extended her medical leave through October. Hoping that time would indeed heal, Amberle made an appointment with her optometrist.

We hoped Dr. Bank would be able to improve what little of Amberle's sight remained with another scleral lens. However, he was disappointingly honest at her appointment.

"The scleral lens will press on the drainage tube. It's out of the question, Amberle."

"You mean, because I had glaucoma surgery, I can't wear a lens to correct the eyesight I have left?"

"I'm sorry," Dr. Bank said. "It won't work." Dr. Bank had worked tirelessly with Amberle over the past few months to make her vision as viable as possible. Now, it looked as if they were at a dead end. Dr. Bank thought for a moment, then looked at Amberle, "There is one thing."

Amberle and Hunter listened as Dr. Bank described another type of lens known as the PROSE®. "It's custom-made to the shape of your eye. Perhaps they could work around the location of the tube. I don't know. I usually don't recommend it because of the price." Amberle and Hunter waited. "It costs around twenty-thousand dollars. And there's no guarantee it will work."

"But it's possible, right?" Amberle asked.

Dr. Bank offered a half-hearted nod. "It's usually not covered by insurance."

"Been there, done that," replied Amberle, remembering the uninsured surgeries miraculously paid for by Tricare. "It's worth a shot."

Amberle and Hunter researched the PROSE® lens, and after discovering its potential, called Dee and me to talk about it.

"I'll speak to Tricare, and we'll make an appointment regardless," Dee said. "Anything is worth a try."

Amberle's case manager at Tricare said the insurance company could provide some small, partial payments for a few of the appointments.

The next available appointment for a PROSE® fitting was in three weeks, and throughout the interim, I fought the temptation to hope in human hands rather than heavenly ones. I asked others to pray for us, focusing on a promise found in 2 Corinthians 1:10–11a (NIV): "He has delivered us from such a deadly peril and he will deliver us again. On him we have set our hope that he will continue to deliver us, as you help us by your prayers."

During the third week of October 2014, I met Amberle in Dallas, and we flew to Houston for the series of appointments. We assumed that since the PROSE® lens was developed specifically for people with corneal anomalies, Amberle's case would not be too unusual. The doctor's initial reaction proved us wrong.

"You're quite the conundrum," he sighed.

Amberle braved four days of examinations and fittings. When she tried on her custom lens, it eased the pain but did nothing for her vision.

"Maybe I need a stronger prescription," Amberle said. "What's the correction now?"

"Correction?" the doctor asked. "You wanted lenses with a correction?"

Somehow, the degree of correction in the lens had not been included in the final paperwork. Over the four-day period, Amberle had seen a myriad of physicians and technicians, and the requirement for a lens that provided both correction and comfort had been changed to comfort only.

"We'll have to remake your lens with the proper specifications. Of course, we won't charge you for this first one."

That's mighty generous of you. "We leave town today at four o'clock," I protested.

"I'm sorry. We'll mail it to you via Fed Ex, and your optometrist can check the fit."

Twenty-thousand dollars of frustration.

When Dr. Bank fitted Amberle with the lenses in Dallas a few days later, they were both pleased. Amberle had less pain and was able to see shapes and shadows. This was a big deal. Shapes and shadows aren't darkness.

We continued to fight for every bit of vision possible. We thought we were doing the right thing, and in a way, we were, but years later, we realized we weren't just fighting blindness; we were fighting God.

We tried to take control of the situation by doing something—anything—to get rid of the difficulty and, as so often happens, our actions created an idol. Something we wanted and we worshiped more than God. Healing.

No, we didn't toss our jewelry into a fire to make a golden calf like the Israelites (Exodus 32), and I didn't tell my husband to sleep with my slave in order to start a family (Genesis 16), but because we couldn't figure out how God could ever work through this situation, we tried to fix it on our own—through prayers, surgeries, exams, and experiments.

Mind you, nothing is wrong with any of these solutions. God uses them all. The problem was our attitude. We craved Amberle's healing more than we craved God. At least, I did. I wanted easy, not hard. And yet, God had already answered our prayer and provided an answer to every question, but I was too busy worshiping the idol of ability to see it.

Late one Monday afternoon, Amberle decided to walk to Whole Foods for a snack. Tired of being on disability, frustrated by her reliance on others, and desiring independence more than food, Amberle knew this twenty-minute walk—her first journey alone since being diagnosed with glaucoma—would be a major accomplishment. Because of the incoming clouds, the Dallas weather was cooler than usual, and Amberle decided it was a perfect opportunity to navigate the outside world using her new white cane. Amberle and Kathryn shopped at Whole Foods several times a week, so Amberle knew the route well. She just had to interpret the directions and the distance in terms of walking rather than driving. She'd take a left out of the front gate, then after a few blocks, another left on . . . what was the name of that street? She couldn't remember right now but knew she'd recognize it when she came to it. From there, it was a straight shot, no more than half a mile. The shopping center was on the right, just before the Central Expressway.

The wind blew Amberle's hair as she left the safety of the apartment complex. Hearing thunder in the distance, she walked briskly. The five-minute drive couldn't be more than a twenty-minute walk. Exiting the apartment complex, Amberle turned left. When she reached the third intersection, she squinted to read the street sign but couldn't make out any of the letters. The location didn't look familiar, so she continued a block further before turning left. Cars whisked by, and the rain fell gently. Amberle didn't mind. It was good to be on her own, even if she was a little wet.

A clap of thunder startled her, and she wished she had her umbrella. When she stepped off the curb to cross the street, her foot slipped on some gravel. Amberle braced her fall with her free hand and landed butt-first on the street. She scrambled to the safety of the sidewalk. Blood trickled down the back of her leg, and her hand ached. Looking for a place to regroup, Amberle realized she was in an unfamiliar area, and she had no idea how to get to Whole Foods or her apartment. Amberle took out her phone. The battery had less than five percent of its charge left. Kathryn was at work and Hunter was at least half an hour away. She called Hunter's number. It went directly to voicemail. After a deep breath to calm herself, she tried again. Nothing.

She uttered a two-word prayer: "God, please."

A few minutes later, her phone vibrated. It was Hunter. "Hey, I saw you called a couple of times, so I—"

Fearing her battery would die, Amberle interrupted. "I . . . I took a walk, and I don't know where I am. I think I'm lost. Can you come get me?"

"Where are you?"

"I told you. I don't know. Please, help me."

"Can you make out anything in the area? A store? A street sign?"

"No, I was walking to Whole Foods, and I got lost. And my phone's about to die."

"OK. Stay where you are. I'll send someone to get you. I'm more than an hour away, but I'll have someone pick you up."

Amberle began to cry. "I . . . I'm on a corner."

"OK. Good. We'll find you. Just stay where you are."

Amberle's screen went dark. Like her world.

She stood on the corner, humiliated and obedient to Hunter's last words. No one stopped to ask why this person with a white cane was standing in the rain with a bloody leg.

"Really, God?" Amberle fumed under her breath. "Really?"

After about ten minutes, Amberle heard one of the passing cars slow down. The driver honked its horn.

"Am?" It was Ali, a friend of Amberle's and Hunter's. "Stay right there," she shouted over the traffic. "I'm making a U-turn."

Ali helped Amberle into her car. "Here, use these towels. Let's get you dry, and I'll take you home."

Amberle's voice quivered. "I'm sorry, Ali."

"Hey, that's what friends are for. No problem."

Ali pulled her car up to the breezeway leading to Amberle's apartment. "Do you need any help?"

"Obviously, Ali, I do. I do need help, but not right now." As Amberle got out of the car, her tears blended with the rain trickling down her face. "Thanks, Ali. You've helped enough for one day. I can get into the apartment on my own."

†

When Amberle called us three days later, she sounded pensive. "Mom, Dad, you said you'd support me whatever I decide, right?"

"Of course, honey," we said together.

"Well, I've made a decision." Amberle spoke slowly as she told us about her experience getting lost in the storm. After she finished, Dee and I groped for words.

"Oh, honey. I can't imagine."

"I'm so sorry."

"It scared me, but I think it knocked some truth into me too. For over a year, we've fought blindness in every way we could. And I'm grateful for your help. But I'm ready to face reality. I'm tired of trying to be who I was, and I'm ready to be who I am. I've signed up for Braille lessons with the Dallas Assistive Rehabilitative Services Department and made an appointment with a specialist from Tarrant County who can help me get the resources I need. I have to start living as a blind person." Amberle waited for our reaction, but Dee and I were consumed with our own thoughts. "I'm sorry. It feels like I've failed, but deep down, I know that's not true. God didn't answer our prayer the way we wanted for me to be healed. But I believe He did answer our prayer. With a no."

Amberle was right. No is a direction—a direction I usually didn't want to go, but a direction nonetheless. Now, *no* meant we had to let go of the old to grasp the new. To hang mid-air, waiting for God to send us a trapeze.

"I'll call the hospital and let them know I won't be coming back to work."

With those words, suddenly, I wasn't just hanging in mid-air. I was spinning out of control. Although they were fully reasonable and somewhat expected, "I won't be coming back to work" sounded sharp and final. Like a death of dreams.

I remembered something Amberle had shared with me several weeks ago. At the time, we didn't know what to make of it, but it made sense now. Amberle had been praying for healing when she sensed the Lord saying, "Why do you pray for healing? I offer resurrection." She wondered if God was chastising her for a lack of faith, so she repented even though it seemed strange to ask forgiveness for praying for healing, especially considering the biblical examples. But now, in light of Amberle's decision to let go of her desire to serve as a nurse and permit the death of her dream, the words seemed prophetic.

For the believer, death is the door to resurrection—to new life. In 2 Corinthians 1:9 (NIV), Paul exhorts believers, "Indeed, we felt we had received the sentence of death. But this happened that we might not rely on ourselves but on God, who raises the dead." Was God giving Amberle a new direction by using the death of one dream to birth another? Forcing us into faith by solely relying on Him?

Amberle could still study public health, but she would do it *with* her blindness, not in spite of it. By accepting her disability, she now envisioned her education as a tool to be used by God rather than a stepping-stone to an earthly objective.

Until now, I'd always believed the ultimate demonstration of a person's faith involved a miraculous event like a supernatural healing or an escape from an impossible situation like David defeating Goliath or Moses at the Red Sea. A remarkable result. Now, I saw something even more amazing—it wasn't the experience that was the ultimate reward; it was the impetus, the individual's total reliance on God. Trusting so completely in God's love, mercy, and grace, the result was almost inconsequential.

I thought of Hebrews 11, the "hall of faith." Great men and women of God who believed and acted in faith: Abraham, Noah, David, and so many others "who through faith conquered kingdoms, enforced justice, obtained promises, stopped the mouths of lions" (Hebrews 11:33 ESV). All with storybook endings any believer would envy. But then, at the end of chapter eleven, other heroes of faith are mentioned. Heroes with no names. Heroes who were tortured, imprisoned, impoverished, and afflicted. It wasn't the result that made them heroes; it was their relationship with God.

I knew Scripture didn't promise a trouble-free life to believers, but I still expected God to remove this situation. Amberle, however, had come to peace, regardless of the result. It was rebellious, in a way. She refused to allow the situation to dictate her emotions. By refusing to fight, she had won. Amberle found stability *not* in spite of the storm but because of it.

Over the next few months, Amberle began speaking of her pain as if it was a privilege. She called it "the fellowship of sufferings." The idea came from Paul's letter to the Philippians: "That I may know him, and the power of his resurrection, and the fellowship of his sufferings, being made comfortable unto his death" (Philippians 3:10 KJV). Amberle challenged us with her newfound strength, reminding us that "Jesus suffered, so why shouldn't we?" or saying things like, "I can't embrace God if I reject His ways." I'd never seen anyone rely on God like that. Coming from her, the words weren't trite. They were true.

When hard days came, which was fairly often, Amberle acknowledged the difficulty, the shaking of her faith. But, she said, she wanted to be shaken, so anything not of Christ—frustration, anger, impatience—would be recognized and removed. Amberle was convinced, now more than ever, that even though her calling to be a missionary was probably true, she had twisted it into an idol by focusing more on serving Christ than knowing Him. She would not do that again. Amberle was grieved by the realization of her past mistakes but grateful for God's grace and whatever future He held for her. Not because of what God would do for her, but simply because He was there. That's what she had gained in her fellowship of sufferings.

Amberle mourned the loss of her dreams, but she was convinced disability was not a detour. It was the road. A road of surrender and suffering, but still, a road. With that recognition, Amberle could move ahead, living the promise of Isaiah 42:16 (NIV): "I will lead the blind by ways they have not known, along unfamiliar paths I will guide them; I will turn the darkness into light before them and make the rough places smooth. These are the things I will do; I will not forsake them."

Chapter Twenty-Eight

Beauty from Ashes

Amberle and Hunter were intentional in their relationship and began exploring the possibility of marriage. Their dates ranged from raucous laughter playing charades with friends to deep discussions of faith. Amberle wrote love songs for Hunter, and he created stories he read aloud to her. Sometimes, Hunter left words of encouragement penned on Amberle's bathroom mirror in erasable marker only to be discovered after he'd left for the evening.

One morning, Dee received a call from Hunter. "Mr. Durano, I have something to confess." Dee was curious. "I kissed Amberle." He paused. "I'm sorry."

"Well, I appreciate your honesty, Hunter," Dee said. "Thank you. Just don't put yourself in a tempting situation, OK?"

"Yes, sir."

As their affection for one another grew, so did Amberle's and Hunter's desire for accountability and honesty. Although Amberle was at peace with her visual impairment, she sometimes grew frustrated over the difficulties it caused. One day, after a particularly challenging experience, Amberle blew up—not at anyone in particular—just at the difficulty of life.

In the midst of her implosion, Hunter gently touched Amberle's forearm. "Am, I can't begin to know what you're experiencing. I'm sorry it's been a difficult day. You're frustrated, and I've felt that way too. But you can't always expect things to go your way."

"Why not?" Amberle snapped. "What's wrong with wanting to have my way?"

"Well, Am," Hunter replied, "that's sin."

†

Amberle learned Braille quickly and discovered ways to "see" without using her eyes. Her social worker applied plastic dots on the stove so she could tell where 350 degrees was and taught her more efficient ways of doing household chores and office work by using the sense of touch or hearing rather than sight. Every day was a mixture of challenges and victories, and navigating the world was a lesson in humility. Simple activities like filling a glass of water, determining the denomination of paper money, reading a menu, or watching television required assistance, either from people or technology. Invisible hurdles were everywhere—non-existent to the majority but overwhelming to those living with disabilities. Nowhere was this more noticeable for Amberle than at church.

Church had always been a second home to Amberle, a hallowed haven, a place where she could understand and be understood. With the loss of her vision, however, came a loss of belonging. Even the simple act of worship—a joy ingrained in her heart since infancy—was complicated and arduous. Amberle couldn't read the lyrics projected on the screens at the front of the auditorium, participate in congregational responses, or follow the Scripture reading from the Bible. It wasn't anyone's fault the church wasn't prepared for visually impaired congregants. They just didn't know.

Amberle had enjoyed teaching children's Sunday school, but when she returned to church after losing her vision, the staff encouraged her to take a break from teaching for a while. Instead of working with

Amberle to figure out how she could serve, the staff saw how she couldn't.

The isolation was excruciating. Amberle couldn't see people nod hello to her, and when she didn't respond, they assumed it was because she felt awkward about her disability. Occasionally, when Amberle heard a cheery "hello" nearby, she responded with an equally cheerful greeting, only to discover she wasn't the recipient of the words. It was difficult to recognize the voices of friends unless someone identified themselves before they spoke, which usually didn't happen. Therefore, although surrounded by dozens of Christian brothers and sisters in a place she knew and loved, Amberle felt abandoned.

One day, she stood in the foyer waiting for the service to begin with only the company of her white cane. *Where are all the other people like me—the people with disabilities?*

Amberle realized she'd never noticed people with disabilities at church before. Perhaps she was the only one. Then a question came to mind: *Why aren't there people with disabilities at church?* Before she could ponder the answer, however, she turned the question on herself: *Why haven't I asked that question before?*

At that moment, God planted a seed in Amberle's heart—the impetus of an idea that would take several years to mature. For now, however, her question about where the people with disabilities were was a fleeting thought—an ambiguous impression dismissed for lack of an answer.

†

Eleven months after Amberle's graduation, Hunter called Dee and asked for Amberle's hand in marriage. Amberle felt now, more than ever, she was called to Johns Hopkins University to gain the tools for whatever future God had for her, and Hunter would go with her.

Always the pragmatist, Dee asked, "What about a job? How do you plan to support her?"

Hunter explained he'd recently realized his dream of becoming a golf pro was an idol so, like Amberle, he'd surrendered his dream to the Lord. He felt God might be calling him into the ministry as church planter, an individual who establishes new churches, and he wanted to explore the idea. The salary of a church planting intern was minimal, but Hunter assured Dee he would take care of Amberle in every way, so Dee gave his approval.

Hunter's proposal was nothing short of a fairytale. After an early morning flight to Seattle, he and Amberle went on a scavenger hunt through the city where Amberle discovered various writings and poems professing Hunter's love to her. Eventually, the couple found their way to a ribbon-and-balloon-lined path that led to a beautiful waterfall (complete with a concealed photographer and Amberle's roommate, Kathryn, and Kathryn's boyfriend, Pearce—also hidden in the trees—who had arrived earlier that day to place the romantic rhymes in secret locations per Hunter's instructions).

Hunter got down on one knee and offered Amberle an antique pearl ring—a family heirloom—as an engagement ring. The pearl represented beauty from pain. After all, had Amberle not become ill, she never would have stayed in Dallas and started dating Hunter. Amberle said yes, and the four friends crossed into Canada for a celebratory dinner and returned to Dallas the next day.

The next seven months were a blur—literally and physically. Two weeks after becoming engaged, Amberle underwent the first of four unsuccessful corneal transplants. In January, we visited Christina and Stephen who were working in China, which unfortunately reopened old wounds for Amberle. With that awareness, however, Amberle began to tend to some invisible injuries from her illness as well as her physical ones.

†

Since Amberle could no longer work due to her disability, she applied for Social Security disability benefits. Once again, God proved

His providence when the clerk told Amberle, "You're incredibly lucky. If you had worked one day less at Baylor Hospital, you wouldn't qualify for SSDI, but somehow you managed to work exactly one day more than what's required for disability payments."

In March 2015, Hunter, Amberle, and I visited Baltimore so Amberle could become familiar with the Johns Hopkins campus and complete the paperwork for her accommodations for graduate school. Hunter met with the head of missions for the Baptist Convention of Maryland and Delaware, Pastor Michael Crawford, who was so impressed by Hunter that he hired him on the spot to help with administrative duties at Freedom Baptist Church. With the help of a realtor friend, Amberle and Hunter leased a small apartment in Baltimore they had only visited virtually.

Amberle and Hunter planned a beautiful outdoor ceremony, and Amberle had my wedding dress retooled into a stunning contemporary gown. We organized showers and bridesmaids' activities and even surprised

Amberle with an "extra bridesmaid." Emily, the friend who had stayed with us during Amberle's initial recovery, flew in from Africa to be part of the celebration.

On May 3, 2015, Amberle and Hunter were married. It was both simple and spectacular—a testimony to God's grace and His ability to create beauty from ashes (Isaiah 61:3).

Chapter Twenty-Nine

New Beginnings

Amberle and Hunter's move to Baltimore meant finding a new community. Because of Hunter's job at Freedom Baptist Church, they knew where they would find their spiritual family. Freedom Baptist was a diverse group of Christ followers. Amberle and Hunter were welcomed warmly, and church members didn't seem put off by Amberle's disability. We didn't realize until much later what a special gift that was.

Disability is hard, especially for Christians. It forces us to evaluate what qualities we esteem in others and ourselves, question why we feel awkward around someone who's different, and craft personalized definitions of ability and worth. That's tough because, at some point, most of us realize we've been kidding ourselves. We do hold certain characteristics above others (although we would never say so publicly)—and weakness isn't one of them.

We like to think of ourselves as strong, smart, capable human beings because, after all, we're made in God's image. However, the same is true for every person with a disability—whether that person is born with a disability or acquires a disability during his lifetime. When you realize a person with a disability is as much an image-bearer of God as a person without a disability (sometimes, more so), you start to understand how very little we know about the actual image of God—the One we're called to reflect.

Fortunately, perhaps because of the diversity in Freedom's congregation, Amberle and Hunter's new community treated Amberle no differently than they treated anyone else.

Being welcomed and becoming friends, however, are two different things. As a genuine extrovert, Amberle thrived on relationships, but now, in a new place with new people, making friends was difficult because of her inability to recognize them.

"I hate it," Amberle said. "If I don't recognize someone's voice, I don't know who it is. And if I don't know who it is, I can't have a meaningful conversation. Hunter, I'm blind—and people are afraid of that. Besides, I don't want to always have to wait for the other person to speak first. I want to be . . . friendly."

"You are," Hunter reassured her.

"No, not when I don't know who's there. Making friends without being able to see them is a lot harder than already having friends and knowing their voices."

It was a familiar pain, one Hunter had seen Amberle endure dozens of times. He held her close, knowing he would never understand what Amberle was feeling—not only because he wasn't blind but because Hunter didn't thrive on relationships the way Amberle did. Hunter was friendly, but Amberle loved people.

"How can I help, Am? What can I do?"

"I don't know. It's just so hard. If I knew who was there, I could just be me."

"What if I helped you?"

"What do you mean?"

"What if I told you who's in the room or who's coming toward us . . . at least until you get familiar with their voices. I could say something like 'Mary at ten o'clock.'"

Amberle laughed. "You'd hate that, Hunter. It's so not you."

"I know. But it is you. So, let's try it."

The next Sunday at church, Hunter and Amberle executed their plan.

"Jo Ann's walking toward us at three o'clock. Mike's coming too." For Hunter, it was awkward, like a cross between being a ventriloquist and an FBI agent. However, when Hunter saw his wife's joy at being able to be friendly again, he didn't care what it felt like.

Forming new relationships in the classroom was more intimidating. The enemy shamed Amberle for her blindness, trying to make her believe her cohort would label her as inferior because of her disability. Fortunately, however, the MSN/MPH program (master of science in nursing/master of public health) incorporated multiple team projects which gave Amberle the opportunity to develop genuine relationships with her peers. With every academic and social success, Amberle grew more confident in her abilities and her calling.

Physically, Amberle's sight continued to deteriorate despite having some of the best vision specialists in the world on her team. During her time in Baltimore, Amberle received three corneal transplants, two of which were emergency surgeries and all of which failed, plus multiple other procedures aimed at saving her vision. Amberle's pain increased significantly, and the whites of her eyes were often bright red. Some days, Hunter came home to find Amberle curled up in a fetal position, praying for sleep to relieve her pain.

During her second semester at Johns Hopkins, Amberle served as an intern with World Relief—a Christian NGO (non-governmental organization) that creates sustainable change through partnerships with local churches. The experience confirmed Amberle's heart for the hurting world, and she longed to know God's plan.

Amberle and Hunter fasted and prayed, asking God to reveal the path He had for Amberle after graduation, but God was silent.

"I just want to know what He wants me to do so I can do it.".

That made perfect sense to us, but God had more to teach us about trust—not only about His will, but about His timing. So, God stayed quiet.

†

Watching Amberle struggle, enduring physical suffering and emotional hardship almost every day, was heartbreaking. Discouragement threatened to steal her joy, but Amberle hung onto hope like a lifeline, fully surrendered to God regardless of the difficulty. I, on the other hand, stubbornly refused to let go of my desire for healing and insisted God do it.

To some Christians, my behavior—my strength and determination—was admirable. But my motivation was wrong. My prayers for healing were based on selfish desires instead of submission to God. I refused to give up my request for restoration and begged God to return Amberle's health to the way it was before, I thought I was praying for healing. But I was wrong.

Healing doesn't mean going back to the way things were before. Healing means moving forward, integrating whatever change has occurred in your life, and moving on from there.

For me, the question of Amberle's healing went straight to my idea of who God is. Disability and divinity seem so at odds. God is good and loving, but God permits and possibly even ordains disability. I needed to find peace in this paradox.

†

One day, at a routine checkup (if there was such a thing for her), Amberle's doctor told her it was time for a change.

"It's too dangerous, Amberle. You've had over twenty surgeries, including four transplants, with no improvement. We can't continue to operate because if something goes wrong now, you could end up in total darkness. Ten percent vision in one eye is better than none at all. Your left eye is non-functioning, and if the pain is too much for you, we can replace it with a glass eye. But it's your call. I just don't see your vision getting any better."

The news would have sent most twenty-somethings into a tailspin, but for Amberle, it confirmed where her hope was—not in a cure, but in Christ. When she told Dee and me the prognosis, she sounded relieved. "At least now I can move forward rather than spending my energy trying to fix something that can't be fixed."

But Dee and I weren't willing to give up.

One afternoon, I sat down to pray, ready to journal what I heard from the Lord. I closed my eyes and asked, "Lord, what do you want?" The words that tumbled onto my paper changed my life.

> *Child, you come to me today wanting answers, but the answer is already here. You cannot see it because you are looking in the wrong place. Healing is not the answer. I am. You have become so focused on your request for healing that it has become an idol. Your desire for healing is greater than your desire for me. Change your focus. Release your request and trust me. I am your answer.*

I read the words I had written. They were not mine. They were His. And they were true.

†

My prayers for Amberle's healing, in and of themselves, weren't sinful, but my motivation was.

That's the trap of idolatry. We want something—a job, a family, financial freedom, health—all perfectly natural desires. Nothing is wrong with any of them—until, one day, our personal desires usurp our desire to know God. Or perhaps it's something we're afraid of, and that fear becomes our focus. I'd fallen into that trap too. Either way, when we spend more time thinking or praying about something other than God Himself, that thing becomes an idol.

So much of the model of Christian prayer involves God answering our requests. God does want us to depend on Him and to bring our requests to Him. He wants us to know He can and will answer our prayers—and He will always cause everything to "work together for the good of those who love God" (Romans 8:28 NLT). Therefore, much of the Christian conversation revolves around God answering prayers—as if the main purpose of prayer is just that. We scatter in a few elements like adoration, confession, and thanksgiving in order to get on God's good side, but most people pray for one reason: to get an answer. After all, we're human, and we want what we want.

However, Ephesians 3:20 (NIV) reminds us God can give us "immeasurably more than all we ask or imagine." In other words, God can give us more than an answer to prayer; He can give us Himself.

That is the purpose of prayer.

I asked God to forgive me for using prayer as a vehicle to accomplish my desires rather than His and for caring more about the results of prayer than my relationship with Him.

His response astounded me.

God didn't make me feel like a failure. He didn't shame me or blame me.

God loved me, and that was the answer I needed.

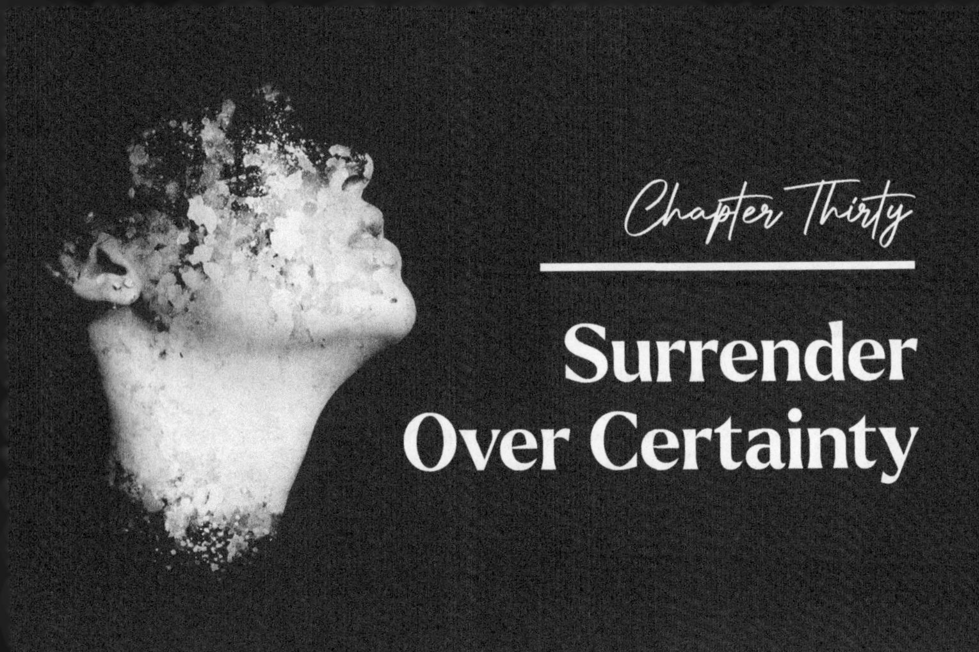

Chapter Thirty

Surrender Over Certainty

I had the answer, but now I had to live it out—especially with regard to letting go of the idol of Amberle's healing.

Daily, I made a choice to direct my thoughts to what I did know rather than what I didn't, but the endless questions and unidentified answers sometimes sucked the life out of me. Ironically, when I stumbled into the abyss of anguish, it was a question that brought me back to reality: "Do you want answers more than you want Jesus?"

Of course, I wanted Jesus more, but like so many things, knowing the answer was one thing; living it was another.

It had been four years since Amberle entered the hospital and four years of unanswered questions. I was starting to be at peace with the absence of answers until one day, during a family phone call, Amberle asked us a question. It came in the form of a prayer request, but when I heard her words, I knew it was much more.

"Mom and Dad, for years now, we've prayed for God to heal my eyes, and God hasn't answered that prayer. I don't know why and I'm not sure I ever will. But lately, I've wondered if maybe God hasn't healed me because . . . He doesn't want me to be healed."

My breathing paused as I processed Amberle's words.

"I don't want to pray against what God wants, so I've been wondering, do you think there's ever a time when a person should stop praying for healing?"

Amberle's words sounded heretical. "What do you mean?"

Amberle repeated her request, choosing her words carefully so Dee and I would understand—but we still didn't. "I want to choose God's way, even if that means I'm blind for the rest of my life. If God doesn't want to heal me, then we need to stop praying for that. Would you pray that I'm sensitive to God's leading?"

Dee muttered something in the affirmative, but when He prayed to close out our phone call, I could tell he was as confused as I was.

The thought of God not wanting to heal Amberle went against everything I knew about God. Just because I no longer held my desire for Amberle's healing as an idol didn't mean I didn't hold it at all. I wanted Amberle to see again, but I also wanted to honor Amberle's request. Throughout the next week, Dee's and my thoughts were held hostage by the idea. Finally, Dee couldn't stand it any longer. "I won't do it. I can't stop praying for her."

"She didn't ask us to stop praying for her," I reminded him. "She asked us to pray that she'd be sensitive to God's plan and that our prayers would line up with God's plan, whatever that is."

"But I know God can heal her."

I knew it too. God was able. But was He willing?

For months, I'd struggled with the meaning of Amberle's journey, eventually concluding that the *why* and the *what* weren't as important as the *Who*. God would use Amberle's pain for His purpose, whatever it was, and my ignorance of that purpose had forced me to trust Him. Now, however, as I considered the possibility of Amberle's blindness being providential, my trust and much of what I believed about God seemed at risk. Amberle's disability made my theology look like an M. C. Escher painting and I didn't know which way was up.

I allowed the idea to envelop me—the thought that God might have ordained Amberle's disability. The belief was incongruous with my theology, and I wondered if it was blasphemous to consider it.

I couldn't wrap my head around the idea of God *causing* one of His children to be disabled, sentencing that child to a life of pain and suffering.

Then I thought about Jesus.

Slowly, I began to understand why I couldn't fathom the idea of God causing Amberle's disability. It was because I'd created God in my own image—a God who wanted me to have a life free of pain and suffering—not a God who invited me into "the fellowship of His sufferings" (Philippians 3:10 NKJV).

I thought about the story in John 9, when Jesus's disciples wanted to know why a man was born blind (John 9:1–12). They thought someone's sin caused it, either the man's or his parents', but Jesus explained, "'Neither this man nor his parents sinned,' said Jesus, 'but this happened so that the works of God might be displayed in him'" (John 9:3 NIV).

Then, I remembered how, in Exodus 4, Moses tried to use his disability, stuttering, as an excuse to not answer God's calling. God wouldn't hear of it: "The LORD said to him, 'Who gave human beings their mouths? Who makes them deaf or mute? Who gives them sight or makes them blind? Is it not I, the LORD? Now go; I will help you speak and will teach you what to say'" (Exodus 4:11–12 NIV). In other words, all ability and disability are under God's sovereignty.

Maybe that was what I needed to know. Whatever God wanted to do through Amberle required her to be disabled, so He orchestrated a consequence of sin in our broken world—disability—for His purpose. God would be glorified through Amberle's blindness. Therefore, He could ordain it. Who was I to say He couldn't?

As I considered Amberle's request, my prayers began to change. Instead of reminding God of my expectations and entitlements, I sat before Him with a single question: "What do *You* want?"

I knew what *I* wanted, but what did God want? When I prayed, I kept my mouth shut and my spirit open. God began to speak, but to my surprise, instead of giving me answers, He reassured me of our relationship. That was what He wanted me to know—that His love surpasses all circumstances and all He wants is me.

The opposite was true as well. All those times I'd searched for answers, I was actually seeking Him. Answers never would have healed my heart, but He could. But I didn't know that yet.

For forty years, I'd exercised my faith by checking boxes—going to church, giving to others, showing kindness. I was a "good Christian." As I discovered this new level of freedom in Christ, however, I realized faith isn't about following rules. It's about knowing and trusting Jesus. God doesn't love me because I'm a good kid; God loves me because I'm His kid. And prayer isn't about getting results; it's about gaining a deeper relationship.

Of course, I knew all that in my head. I'd read it, sung about it, and even told others about it, but I had a hard time living it. I equated God's affection with His blessings, and now I saw how foolish that was. Blessings aren't proof of God's love. Blessings are proof of God's character.

This revelation—that God doesn't *primarily* show His love through circumstances but proves it through relationship—provided the peace I needed to let go of my fears regarding Amberle's disability. I could pray freely, without the fear of hearing an answer I didn't like. I knew I was loved, and I could rely on assurance instead of answers.

Chapter Thirty-One

More than an Answer

A few weeks later, through God's providence, a friend and I attended a "Fresh Grounded Faith" conference featuring Jennifer Rothschild—an author, speaker, and Bible study leader who is blind. Right before the afternoon break, ushers distributed notecards to attendees so we could submit questions to Jennifer. This is a common practice at women's conferences in order to give the audience an "up close and personal" time with the speaker. Jennifer said the topics could range from silly to spiritual and that certainly included questions regarding her disability.

My stomach churned as I slowly wrote the question on my heart: *My daughter lost her vision several years ago. We have been praying for her healing, but God has not answered our prayer. Do you feel there is ever a time when a person should stop praying for healing from a disability?* I placed my notecard into a basket with all the other cards and immediately wanted to take it back, but before I could, several other ladies placed their cards on top of mine.

All I could do was pray. *Lord, please don't let her choose my card.* Why was I so afraid of getting an answer—one answer to one of a million questions?

After the break, Jennifer's husband, Phil, drew questions out of the basket and read them aloud. A few questions addressed the topics Jennifer had taught about earlier that day, but many of the questions were about her disability: how she put on makeup, chose outfits, or fixed dinner. Jennifer answered each one thoughtfully. Then, I heard the words I'd written, "My daughter lost her vision several years ago . . ." My throat tightened, and my friend who was sitting next to me grabbed my hand. When Phil finished reading the question, he let out an audible sigh. All eyes were on Jennifer.

"Oh, friend," Jennifer began, "being blind is hard, and I do believe people should pray for healing. But it's difficult because sometimes people get healed, and sometimes they don't. And we don't know why." The compassion in her voice was palpable. "What's important here is that we not only pray for healing, but we pray for other things as well—things like joy, peace, and contentment." Jennifer spoke about the importance of spiritual well-being over physical wholeness and explained how a person could be physically healed but spiritually wounded by bitterness, anger, and jealousy. "Pray for contentment above healing. That will make a huge difference. God has a purpose for your daughter's pain; it just hasn't been revealed yet. Prayer for healing is important but pray for contentment first."

There was my answer in a word: contentment.

After the conference, attendees had the opportunity to meet Jennifer. I waited in line, and when the time came, I reached out to shake Jennifer's hand and quietly revealed my identity, "I'm the person who wrote the question about my daughter being blind."

She immediately embraced me. "I want you to know something," she said, releasing me from her bear hug but grasping my hands. "Being blind is harder on the parent than it is on the child. As a mom or a dad, you just want to save your child, but you can't, and it's horrible because you feel so helpless." Tears filled her sightless eyes as well as mine. "It's always more painful to watch someone you love go through suffering than to go through it yourself. You'd trade places with your daughter in a minute because that's what love is. And that's exactly what Jesus did . . . for me, for you, and for your daughter. I promise, her pain has a purpose." Jennifer sighed as if a vital message had been delivered, then she smiled and said, "Tell me about your daughter."

After a short conversation, Jennifer prayed for me and recorded a video message on my phone to Amberle.

It was more than an answer.

†

For years, I'd waited for God to bless Amberle—to heal her, to show His love to her through some miraculous healing. I thought I could never be content without that specific blessing, without that answer. Ironically, it was my search for answers that made me spiritually blind, unable to see that God had already provided every answer I'd ever need. But first, I had to discover God doesn't prove His love through circumstances. God proved His love by establishing a relationship with us when we were completely undeserving (Romans 5:8). He doesn't demonstrate His love by His blessings; He gives us His blessings because of His love—because of who He is, not because of who I am.

I couldn't find the answer because I already had it.

The more I thought about it, the more I realized Amberle's disability didn't mean God didn't love her. It meant God *did* love her. He gave her a gift to be stewarded for a purpose we didn't yet know. And we had to trust Him for that purpose.

Slowly, I began to let go of my insistence for Amberle's healing, and as I did, something began to let go of me. The chains of worry, fear, and stress I'd forged by insisting on my own way crumbled. I was breaking free from the lie of needing to know why and could trust God without demanding an answer.

As Amberle's graduation approached, the uncertainty of her future grew. So did Amberle's frustration. After all, she and Hunter had left everyone and everything they'd known in Texas to follow God—for Amberle to get a degree in public health to fulfill what she felt was a calling from God. But now, God was silent. Amberle applied for jobs out of necessity but felt no passion.

At the suggestion of her advisor, Amberle attended the Christian Connections for International Health Conference in Washington, DC. "You'll be exposed to multiple areas of public health, and hopefully, at the conference, you can do some networking and find an area you can focus on."

Amberle perused the conference schedule on the train to Washington, trying to decide which breakout sessions to attend. All the programs seemed engaging, but her attention was piqued by a session called "A Pathway to Health for the Disabled," a breakout that promised to address disability inclusion in churches around the world. Although Amberle had lived with disability for four years, she was unfamiliar with the concept of disability inclusion as a field of public health.

The words she heard in that session changed her life: "People with disabilities, if they were counted as a single people group, would be the largest unreached population in the world. Over one billion people worldwide live with disabilities, and fewer than ten percent of that population will ever hear an effective presentation of the gospel. Even in America, approximately one in four individuals is physically, intellectually, or developmentally disabled, but we don't see that ratio in our churches." The speakers discussed the importance of disability inclusion in both healthcare and the church and showcased several organizations having a positive impact around the world.

Amberle's heart pounded as she listened to the speakers—professionals who had merged their passion for Christ, their knowledge of healthcare, and their love for people into one glorious goal: disability inclusion. She was intrigued by the information and passionate about the cause, but mostly, Amberle was overwhelmed by the faithfulness of God who, at that moment, was calling her to serve people with disabilities.

Returning to Baltimore, Amberle could hardly contain herself as she told Hunter about God answering her prayer.

"Am, that's amazing!" said Hunter. "This is about so much more than a career field. All your life you've had a heart to reach people for Christ. You knew you'd be most effective with people who are like you, so you asked for something impossible, to be an indigenous missionary to an unreached people group." Tears streamed down both of their faces. "When God made you blind, he also made you an indigenous missionary to the world's largest unreached people group—people with disabilities. Am, this is the answer to *that* prayer!"

It was true. More than anything, Amberle wanted to serve an unreached people group, and research said the most effective missionaries were people who were indigenous to that group. Amberle was an upper-middle-class Filipino-American—and no amount of prayer could transform her into a person of an unreached, ethnic heritage. But now, after twenty-four years of waiting, God had directed her toward her calling in less than twenty-four hours: disability inclusion.

When Amberle told Dee and me about how God had revealed Himself to her, we were ecstatic.

"What the devil intended for bad, God intended for good," said Dee, alluding to the story of Joseph in Genesis 50.

Amberle asked us to not tell any of our friends what had happened until she had a job. "I want to make sure God leads me—not some human connection."

Several weeks went by. Amberle investigated multiple NGOs, but sadly, disability inclusion wasn't standard practice among them. "There's a lot of need, Mom, but very few opportunities."

"We'll keep praying. I'm sure God will lead you to the right place."

About a month before graduation, Amberle and Hunter were leaving a prayer meeting at Freedom Church when their pastor, Michael Crawford, called out to them. "Hey, Am and Hunter, do you guys have a minute?"

"Sure, Pastor Mike. What do you need?"

Pastor Mike hesitated, unusual for a man of his confidence. He was a dynamic leader in the Southern Baptist Convention, and served both as lead pastor of Freedom Church in Baltimore and director of missions for the Baptist Convention of Maryland and Delaware.

Pastor Mike took a breath. "You guys are going to think I'm crazy, but God has given me a vision, and I'm supposed to talk to you about it, Amberle."

"Me?"

He nodded. "In my work at BCMD, I've been studying unreached people groups, and there's a lot of research about people with disabilities being the largest unreached population in the world. God's given me a vision to start an organization—a resource for churches that need information and assistance when they have a question about serving people with disabilities or when they want to start a disability ministry."

Amberle couldn't believe what she was hearing.

"I know you're getting ready to graduate, Amberle, and I don't know if you have a job or not, but I was wondering if you'd be interested in helping me start this organization and make this vision a reality. It'd be a volunteer position for now, but we might be able to get some grants next year. Anyway, I don't know if you're interested in doing this, but God told me to tell you about it, so I am."

"I don't believe it," said Hunter. Then he laughed. "Actually, I do."

When Amberle explained what God had been doing in her life and how she felt called to disability inclusion, all three of them realized it was a match made in heaven. Amberle agreed to start the following week by researching similar organizations to find out what was needed and make sure they weren't duplicating the efforts of other nonprofits.

†

On December 16, 2016, Amberle graduated with an MSN/MPH from Johns Hopkins University—and a 4.0 GPA. I held back tears while watching her cross the stage, doing what many thought was impossible.

Amberle still didn't have a job, but no one doubted she was right where she needed to be. Amberle had enjoyed researching disability-related NGOs on behalf of the fledgling organization, and seeing the need for such a resource fueled her passion for the cause.

"Most organizations help churches develop services for family members," she said, "like a special needs class for kids or a respite night for parents. That's good but it's obligatory. Special needs ministry doesn't have the same status as youth ministry or children's ministry, when churches try to be creative and use the program as a tool for outreach. Most churches see disability ministry as a service, almost like babysitting, rather than a necessity. There's a whole mindset shift that needs to take place—an appreciation for people with disabilities and a recognition that people with disabilities are a vital part of the church." Amberle's enthusiasm was contagious.

"We'll call the organization The Banquet Network, based on the parable in Luke 14 where the Master invites all his neighbors to a banquet. Most of them give excuses why they can't come, so the Master tells His servants to go out and bring in the poor, the crippled, the lame, and the blind (Luke 14:13). On the surface, it looks like the Master is just trying to fill His table, and He is, but there's more to it. Unlike the Great Commission (Matthew 28:16–20), when Jesus tells his followers to *go* and make disciples of all nations, this parable teaches we should actually *bring in* people with disabilities. It's a huge difference. Jesus wants people with disabilities in the Church because that's the only way the body of Christ will be complete. The Banquet Network will empower churches to do that."

†

As a graduation celebration, Dee and I had planned a short trip to New York with Amberle and Hunter. Christina and Stephen surprised us by flying in from China to join us, so I was elated. While we were chatting on the train to New York, Amberle received a phone call. "I think I'll answer this. It's Brandon, my former supervisor at World Relief." She moved to a quieter area of the train.

During her second semester of graduate school, Amberle had served as an intern at World Relief—a Christian NGO that partners with churches around the world to fight poverty, violence, and injustice. The experience had confirmed her desires early on, and she was eager to share her new direction.

"Congratulations, Amberle," Brandon said. "We were talking about you the other day, and if we've calculated correctly, you've just graduated."

"That's right," Amberle said.

"What are your plans? Do you have a job lined up?"

"Well, I don't have a job yet, but I definitely have plans." Amberle shared about her passion for disability inclusion and The Banquet Network.

"That's amazing, and everything you've said confirms that God put you on my mind today for a reason. We were talking about individuals who might be interested in joining our team at World Relief, and your name came up." Brandon began to describe a position that Amberle had dreamed of—a public health professional based in Baltimore who would serve marginalized people groups through World Relief. The position included annual training trips to other countries. "What do you think, Amberle? Are you interested?"

"Interested? It's a dream job! But . . . I'm not sure I'm qualified. I mean, I did just graduate, and I don't have that much practical experience. Plus, God did some extraordinary things to get me to The Banquet Network, so I think that's where I need to be, even if it is just a volunteer position for now."

"I do believe God's called you to The Banquet Network, Amberle, and I never want to interfere with God's work. But it sounds like you need something to pay the bills, and a job at World Relief would do that. What if we could work out a schedule where you could work at both places?"

Amberle couldn't believe what she was hearing. "I . . . I would pray about it."

"Good. Let's leave it at that. You pray about it, and we will too. Let's talk next week. Enjoy your time with your family."

When Amberle returned to us, we were curious about the phone call. "What did he want?"

"He wanted to congratulate me."

"Oh, that's nice."

"And he offered me a job!"

"What?"

Amberle recapped the conversation.

"That's amazing, Amberle," said Christina. "What are you going to do?"

"Well," she smiled, "first, I'm going to pray."

"Let's all do that," Dee said. Together, we thanked God for this blessing of opportunity and asked for wisdom and discernment for Amberle and Hunter. Afterward, our conversation turned to our plans in New York, but our hearts were focused on God's faithfulness.

Chapter Thirty-Two

Hope Through Heartache

Several days later, Brandon called Amberle with a job offer from World Relief. He proposed that every other week, Amberle could take Friday to work on The Banquet Network. The idea seemed feasible, so on January 9, 2017, twenty-two operations and four-and-a-half years after experiencing an allergic reaction resulting in toxic epidermal necrolysis, Amberle started working for World Relief. Although her title included words such as *program advisor* and *monitoring and evaluation*, essentially, Amberle was a missionary nurse. When her supervisors realized Amberle's passion for people with disabilities, they allowed her to include disability work as a passion project. Amberle became World Relief's disability point person—and she effectively served as an indigenous missionary nurse to the world's largest unreached people group, people with disabilities. God answered Amberle's prayer not in spite of her disability but because of it.

Looking back now, I see I was willing to settle for so much less than what God wanted to give us. I wanted a one-time healing, but God gave us daily miracles as Amberle navigates the world in her weakness and His strength.

For a long time, I thought disability was the problem. I was wrong. The problem was my reaction to disability and my expectation that a solution could be found in a circumstance and was within my control. That expectation was my limitation. I wanted an answer so I wouldn't have to trust God.

Through His grace, however, I discovered I didn't need an answer. Answers satisfy the head, but relationships heal the heart. My heart was broken, and God used the pain of Amberle's suffering to draw me to Himself.

One thing is certain. God does answer prayer. Every. Single. Time. When the answer is yes, we celebrate, but when the answer is no, the prayer feels unanswered. Even though it isn't.

Romans 8:28 promises "in all things God works for the good of those who love him, who have been called according to his purpose." That good, however, according to Romans 8:29, is being "conformed to the image of his Son" (NIV). When God reshapes our heart and teaches us to embrace our weaknesses, we can witness from our wounds. Like Jesus.

Although Amberle is not physically healed today, her journey brought healing to many, including me. God trusted us with His answer and used what hurt us to heal us—not to return us to the way things were, but to move us forward to a life that is "more than we can ask or imagine" (Ephesians 3:20). Healing doesn't look the way I thought it would, but then, things never do with God.

If you're in the midst of heartache, I'm sorry. Press into God, and let Him carry you through the pain. You won't find hope *in* the heartache, but you can find hope *through* it—because you are not alone. God can use the very thing you wish didn't exist as a catalyst for faith—if you trust Him.

The faith God gives you for an "unanswered" prayer can take you beyond heartache to hope. But, as Paul reminds us, we must "fix our eyes not on what is seen, but on what is unseen, since what is seen is temporary, but what is unseen is eternal" (2 Corinthians 4:18).

Will you do that? Will you let go of your need for answers and "walk by faith, not by sight" (2 Corinthians 5:7)? God is faithful. Let Him to take you beyond what you can see and transform your faith into sacred sight.

EPILOGUE

If this book has touched your heart or challenged your ideas regarding disability inclusion and the Church, I encourage you to search the Scriptures for God's truth on the matter.

Over one billion people live with disabilities worldwide, and it's estimated that fewer than ten percent of them will ever hear the gospel formally. Approximately one in four Americans is physically, mentally, or developmentally disabled, but we don't see that ratio in our churches. In fact, fewer than twenty percent of American churches offer any sort of disability ministry.

Disability ministry isn't just about ministering *to* people with disabilities. It's about ministering *with* them, recognizing their spiritual gifts and serving side-by-side—because disability inclusion isn't about our differences. It's about our similarities. People with disabilities are not "projects;" they are fellow image-bearers of Christ. We are all one in His body.

The Banquet Network empowers followers of Christ to welcome and integrate individuals and families impacted by disabilities into the life of the local and global Church. They coach churches in establishing a disability ministry based on that specific church's vision and values. The Banquet Network also offers free resources on its website including the *Inspire Curriculum*—a seven-week study for congregations or small groups that examines disability from a gospel perspective.

If you'd like find out more about The Banquet Network or if you want to help integrate disabilities into the life of the Church by supporting The Banquet Network, go to https://www.thebanquetnetwork.com.

†

Amberle served as the executive director of The Banquet Network through 2020. The organization gained notoriety for its outstanding coaching of churches in disability inclusion and outreach and continues to fill a vital role today. In December 2020, Amberle and Hunter moved to Oxford, England, where Hunter began a master of studies and DPhil (doctoral) program in theology. In February 2021, Amberle was hired by Compassion International as a monitoring and evaluation specialist, where she continues to work today.

Because of TEN, doctors gave Amberle little hope for a healthy pregnancy, but after one miscarriage, Amberle delivered a beautiful baby boy in January 2023, Atlas Origen Brown. He is proof of God's redemption—a miracle in the making. At this writing, Amberle is pregnant with another rainbow baby.

Stephen and Christina live in Manila, Philippines, where Christina serves as a supervisory regional development outreach and communications specialist for the U. S. Agency for International Development, and Stephen works as a private investor.

Dee and Glenda live in Rio Rancho, New Mexico. Although Dee still builds homes, they both consider themselves retired, promoted to grandparent status with the opportunity to spend more time with family in Oxford, the Philippines, or wherever the Lord takes them.

Glenda enjoys sharing her faith through writing and speaking and invites people to contact her through glendadurano.com or on social media.

If you found this book meaningful, please post a review on Amazon. Glenda has also written a thirty-day devotional inspired by her family's journey which she hopes will encourage individuals in times of crisis. The devotional, available on Amazon.com, is called *Desperate for God.* (Be sure to add the author's name when searching for it.) To view the blog about Amberle's illness, go to caringbridge.org, click on "find a caring bridge," and search for Amberle Grace Durano.

The proceeds from this book will be donated to The Banquet Network.

Made in the USA
Las Vegas, NV
09 January 2025

16145593R00125